The London Transit System Bombings

Titles in the Lucent Terrorism Library include:

America Under Attack: Primary Sources
America Under Attack: September 11, 2001
Civil Liberties and the War on Terrorism
The History of Terrorism
The Iraqi Prisoner Abuse Scandal
The Patriot Act
Terrorists and Terrorist Groups
The War Against Iraq

THE

LUCENT

TERRORISM

LIBRARY

The London Transit System Bombings

Gail B. Stewart

LUCENT BOOKS

An imprint of Thomson Gale, a part of The Thomson Corporation

Detroit • New York • San Francisco • San Diego • New Haven, Conn. • Waterville, Maine • London • Munich

© 2006 by Lucent Books. Lucent Books is an imprint of The Gale Group, Inc., a division of Thomson Learning, Inc.

Lucent Books® and Thomson Learning™ are trademarks used herein under license.

For more information, contact
Lucent Books
27500 Drake Rd.
Farmington Hills, MI 48331-3535
Or you can visit our Internet site at http://www.gale.com

LIBRARY OF CONGRESS CATALOGING-IN-PUBLICATION DATA

Stewart, Gail, 1949-
The London transit system bombings / by Gail B. Stewart.
p. cm. — (The Lucent terrorism library)
Includes bibliographical references and index.
ISBN 1-59018-933-7 (hard cover : alk. paper) 1. London Terrorist Bombings,
London, England, 2005. I. Title. II. Series.
HV6433.G713L65 2006
942.1'086—dc22

2005032557

Printed in the United States of America

Contents

Foreword

It was the bloodiest day in American history since the battle of Antietam during the Civil War—a day in which everything about the nation would change forever. People, when speaking of the country, would henceforth specify "before September 11" or "after September 11." It was as if, on that Tuesday morning, the borders had suddenly shifted to include Canada and Mexico, or as if the official language of the United States had changed. The difference between "before" and "after" was that pronounced.

That Tuesday morning, September 11, 2001, was the day that Americans began to learn firsthand about terrorism, as first one fuel-heavy commercial airliner, and then a second, hit New York's World Trade Towers—sending them thundering to the ground in a firestorm of smoke and ash. A third airliner was flown into a wall of the Pentagon in Washington, D.C., and a fourth was apparently wrestled away from terrorists before it could be steered into another building. By the time the explosions and collapses had stopped and the fires had been extinguished, more than three thousand Americans had died.

Film clips and photographs showed the horror of that day. Trade Center workers could be seen leaping to their deaths from seventy, eighty, ninety floors up rather than endure the 1,000-degree temperatures within the towers. New Yorkers who had thought they were going to work were caught on film desperately racing the other way to escape the wall of dust and debris that rolled down the streets of lower Manhattan. Photographs showed badly burned Pentagon secretaries and frustrated rescue workers. Later pictures would show huge fire engines buried under the rubble.

It was not the first time America had been the target of terrorists. The same World Trade Center had been targeted in 1993 by Islamic terrorists, but the results had been negligible. The worst of such acts on American soil came in 1995 at the hands of a homegrown terrorist whose hatred for the government led to the bombing of the federal building in Oklahoma City. The blast killed 168 people—19 of them children.

But the September 11 attacks were far different. It was terror on a frighteningly well-planned, larger scale, carried out by nineteen men from the Middle East whose hatred of the United States drove them to the most appalling suicide mission the world had ever witnessed. As one U.S. intelligence officer told a CNN reporter, "These guys turned airplanes into weapons of mass destruction, landmarks familiar to all of us into mass graves."

Some observers say that September 11 may always be remembered as the date that the people of the United States finally came face to face with terrorism. "You've been relatively sheltered from terrorism," says an Israeli terrorism expert. "You hear about it happening here in the Middle East, in Northern Ireland, places far away from you. Now Americans have joined the real world where this ugliness is almost a daily occurrence."

This "real world" presents a formidable challenge to the United States and other nations. It is a world in which there are no rules, where modern terrorism is war not waged on soldiers, but on innocent people—including children. Terrorism is meant to shatter people's hope, to create instability in their daily lives, to make them feel vulnerable and frightened. People who continue to feel unsafe will demand that their leaders make concessions—*do something*—so that terrorists will stop the attacks.

Many experts feel that terrorism against the United States is just beginning. "The tragedy is that other groups, having seen [the success of the September 11 attacks] will think: why not do something else?" says Richard Murphy, former ambassador to Syria and Saudi Arabia. "This is the beginning of their war. There is a mentality at work here that the West is not prepared to understand."

Because terrorism is abhorrent to the vast majority of the nations on the planet, President George W. Bush's declaration of war against terrorism was supported by many other world leaders. He reminded citizens that it would be a long war, and one not easily won. However, as many agree, there is no choice; if terrorism is allowed to continue unchecked the world will never be safe.

The volumes of the Lucent Terrorism Library help to explain the unexplainable events of September 11, 2001, as well as examine the history, personalities, and issues connected with the ensuing war on terror. Annotated bibliographies provide readers with ideas for further research. Fully documented primary and secondary source quotations enliven the text. Each book in this series provides students with a wealth of information as well as launching points for further study and discussion.

The Bloodiest Day

On July 7, 2005, the people of London found that life in a city can change in an instant—or, more accurately, in the span of fifty-seven minutes. It was on that day that four separate bombs went off during the height of the morning rush hour. Three of the bombs exploded within seconds of each other as they ripped through train cars in London's underground railway system. The fourth exploded fifty-seven minutes later, shearing the top from one of the city's double-decker buses. Amid the blood, glass shards, and twisted metal of the four bomb sites, fifty-three people were dead and seven hundred more were injured—many critically. It was the bloodiest day Britain had seen since World War II.

A Range of Effects

Terror and confusion followed as people frantically sought news of loved ones who might have been on the bus or one of the trains. Dublin schoolteacher Tara O'Beirn was in London on July 7 visiting her sister Gillian, an accountant in London's financial district. O'Beirn recalls sitting in a coffee shop and hearing people talking about a bombing.

"It was like one of those times when you're not really listening," she says, "and you just hear it in the corner of your mind, without it really sinking in, you know? I finally looked up from my book and asked someone, 'Are you talking about a bombing here?' And he said, 'Yeah, they've bombed the Underground and a bus—the No. 30.'"

Tara says she had a sinking feeling that the No. 30 bus was the one her sister took to work. "I tried calling her then. I kept trying her mobile phone as well as her phone at work. But it was really frustrating, because the mobile

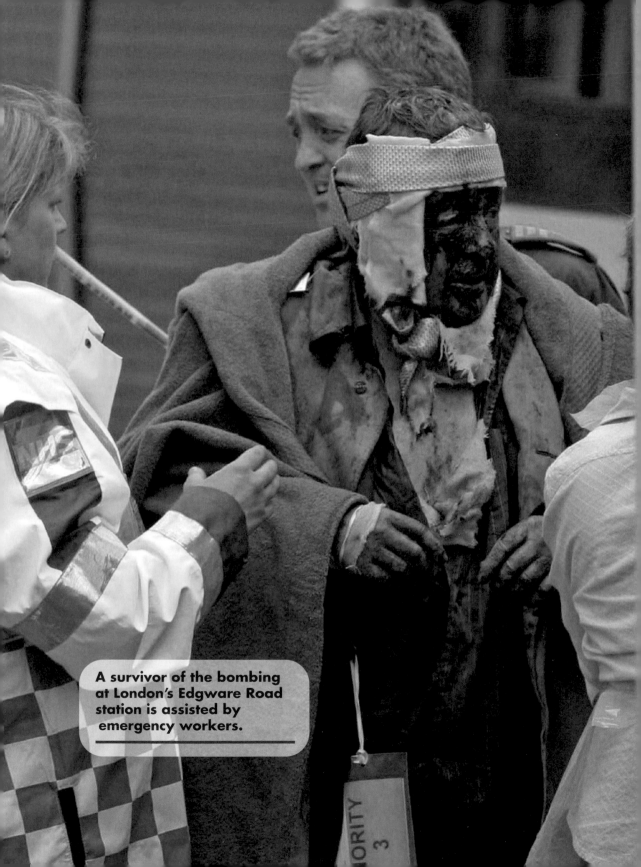

A survivor of the bombing at London's Edgware Road station is assisted by emergency workers.

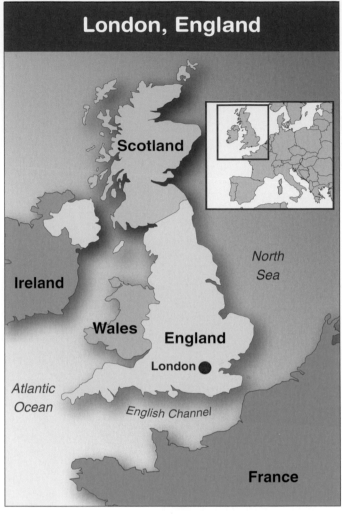

London, England

Scotland

Ireland

Wales

England

London ●

North Sea

Atlantic Ocean

English Channel

France

couldn't reach that morning was a big part of the damage the terrorists did. The not knowing. I wondered if my sister had been on the bus, and if she was dead. Your mind just jumps to the scariest thoughts. For a few hours, everyone in London seemed to be in the same situation, feeling that they'd maybe lost someone, but they weren't sure."[1]

Grief and Fear

The shock waves resulting from the London bombings of July 7 had enormous, wide-ranging negative effects—from the grief of victims' families and the physical and emotional suffering of the injured, to the anxiety and fear felt by Londoners who wondered whether more attacks were imminent. In addition, after fundamentalist Muslims claimed responsibility for the attacks, some members of London's Muslim community became targets of hate crimes by angry Londoners. And finally, the bombings resulted in worry about Britain's economy, especially because tourism is so important to London businesses during the summer months. Would visitors feel safe coming to London for a vacation, people wondered, especially after seeing the news footage of the mangled trains and the double-decker bus, as well

phone lines had been shut down throughout the city so that emergency crews could get through. And I had no better luck with land lines. By that time I was getting really scared.

"Things did turn out all right, though. I finally was able to get through from a phone [booth] to her office. She was fine, and that was a huge relief. I really think that the fear and nervousness people felt about their friends and family members they as the endless stream of ambulances carrying the bodies away?

Strength and Resolve

Remarkably, however, the bombings also highlighted the strength of the people of Britain. Ordinary Londoners acted heroically, many of them risking their own lives to help victims to safety in the moments after the blasts. Medics and rescuers rushed to the scene, calming the wounded though they themselves were frightened and appalled at the carnage around them. The attacks showed the resolve and resourcefulness of London's law enforcement community, too, as police, intelligence officials, and forensic crews accomplished a seemingly impossible investigation in days, rather than weeks or months.

When that fifty-seven minutes was over, Britain had joined the growing list of nations that had been attacked by al Qaeda terrorists —a list that also includes its closest ally, the United States. Though the people of London weathered the terrorist bombings and the frightening days that followed, changes would take place—in security, in mass transit, and even in how the people of London viewed one another. The continuing threat of terrorism meant that for Londoners, just as for the people of the United States after September 11, 2001, things would never be quite the same.

Chapter One

What a Difference a Day Makes

On the morning of July 7, 2005, Londoners were in the mood to celebrate. Only the day before, they had learned that the city had been selected to host the 2012 Olympic Games. Though most experts believed Paris would be chosen by the International Olympic Committee, London was announced as the winner on July 6, and people throughout the city were deliriously happy. The Olympics would bring hundreds of thousands of visitors—and their tourist dollars—to the city. And for the duration of the games—more than two weeks—London would be the focus and envy of every city on Earth.

Sebastian Coe, a former Olympic athlete who helped present London's bid for the games, said the city deserved the honor, announcing simply, "This is our moment."[2] Prime Minister Tony Blair enthusiastically agreed, saying, "Many people do reckon that London is the greatest city in the world at this moment."[3]

The announcement of London's selection set off parties and celebrations throughout the city. "We couldn't believe it," says one university student. "It was supposed to be Paris [that won], and we were pretty resigned to be disappointed. And we heard the news, and we were speechless—for about thirty seconds. And then we were on top of the world. I was so proud to live in this amazing city!"[4]

"I Saw a Silver Light"

Even people who have no connection with the sporting world felt a thrill when their city was chosen as the host of the 2012 Olympics. The excitement could be felt among commuters who made their way to the London Underground stations the following morning. "I was in a bright mood," recalls thirty-nine-year-old banker Michael Henning. "It was a nice morning, we had just got the Olympics. Life is really quite good, I thought to myself."[5]

At about 8:30 A.M. Henning boarded the train at the Aldgate East subway station in London's busy financial district. The train was rapidly filling with passengers, he noted, as he settled in the second car with his newspaper. Shortly after boarding, Henning saw a blinding flash of light. "I saw a silver light, it was flying glass—and then a flash of yellow," he remembers. "I was thrown to the ground and my whole body twisted round. I was lying on my front, my face wet with blood." The rest of the car, he says, went completely dark. "Everyone was panicking and screaming. . . . There was dust, smoke. I knew immediately it was a bomb."[6]

Many of the train's passengers said they did not hear an explosion; they only saw the

Commuters hurry along the platform at King's Cross station in London's Underground.

Experiencing an al Qaeda Bomb

Twenty-one-year-old Katie Benton, an American veterinary student, was traveling on the Edgware Road train with her sister Emily when the bomb went off on July 7. In this excerpt from David Frabotta's article "Surviving London," she describes the experience, which left her with a punctured eardrum and severe cuts and Emily with broken bones in her hand and foot.

"There was debris in the air. The same air that carries the debris carries a heat that caused the sensation like we were being electrocuted. We caught a lot of glass in our face, so our faces were really bloody and we were remarkably dirty. That was the first thing I noticed about Emily. . . .

It happened right as [the train] pulled out of the station. A bomb blast is not a fireball; it doesn't feel anything like it looks in the movies. Everything went black, and it was intensely painful from the heat that emanated from the bomb. Once that feeling stopped and we could open our eyes and look around, the debris had already been blown to where it was going to be blown. When we could open our eyes and look around, we had already sustained all the injuries we were going to."

intense flash. The noise was unmistakable above the Underground line, however. Ken Edwards, who was in his office on the fifth floor of a building nearby, was frightened by the sound, which he later described as "like a great door slamming."[7] As the walls and windows of his building shook, Edwards looked out and saw smoke pouring from the air vents of the Underground.

"It Was a Burnt-Out Shell"

Immediately after the explosion, panic spread through the Aldgate train. The train filled with smoke, and people could not breathe or see. Passenger Mustafa Kurtulda scrambled from her seat in a nearby car and saw immediately that the third car had sustained the heaviest damage. Its walls were charred and black, and the door had been blown off. "It was a burnt-out shell," she says. "There was a body of someone aged about twenty lying there—I couldn't tell if it was a man or woman. Another twenty were lying nearby, their faces cut and bleeding."[8]

Bruce Lait, a dance instructor from Cambridge, was in the third car when the bomb went off. He was one of the only passengers in the car who escaped without critical injuries. Lait says the explosion occurred only moments after the train began moving: "We'd been on there for a minute at most and then something happened. It was like a huge electricity surge which knocked us out and burst our eardrums." When he regained consciousness a few minutes later, he realized that there was a dead body on top of him.

With his face bleeding, Lait was helped from the car by police and paramedics. "It was just the most awful scene of death and there were body parts everywhere,"[9] he says.

A Second Blast

Within seconds of the Aldgate explosion, another bomb went off on a train leaving the Edgware Road station. The bomb blew a large crater in the floor of the car and tore through the wall, hitting a train that was headed in the opposite direction on an adjacent track.

Passengers at Edgware Road were immediately plunged into darkness and smoke.

Some quickly turned on their cell phones and took pictures of the chaos and destruction. Others tried to assess the injuries of those around them. Several of the dead lay on the tracks between the two trains. The cries and screams of the injured and dying victims could be heard throughout the train. As one passenger later recalled, "Somebody, a man I think, was blown out of the door of the train—he was under the carriages. . . . The screams from the guy who was under the train made the whole incident so much worse."[10]

French architect Nicolas Thioulouse was on the train adjacent to the bombed train.

This mobile phone photograph taken by a passenger just after a bomb exploded on the train he was on shows the devastation inside the train car.

He too heard the screams. "The sound of people crying and shouting for help was just horrible. I never felt so unpowerful in my life." What he saw, however, was nearly as bad as what he had heard. "I had the feeling I was in a fish tank," he says, "seeing people in the opposite car with their faces completely covered by blood."[11]

"I'm Dying on an Underground Train"

Seven people were killed on the Aldgate train, and another seven on the Edgware Road train. As horrible as the death and injury tolls were, experts said that it could have been far worse had the trains been further underground. In both instances the force of the blast was spread over a fairly wide tunnel. The third blast, however, could not have occurred in a worse place.

The bomb went off on a Piccadilly Line train soon after it left King's Cross station. The packed train had just descended into a narrow tunnel that was 60 feet (20m) below the streets of London. The blast went off in the first car, but passengers several cars removed were knocked from their seats by the explosion.

"It happened in an instant," says Australian passenger Gill Hicks, who lost both legs in the explosion, "less time than it takes to snap your fingers." She later recalled how completely dark it was, and how frightened people around her were when they realized that the smoke and dust were

In this photo taken by a passenger with his mobile phone camera, survivors of the bombings make their way to safety through a smoky tunnel.

July 7 Bombings

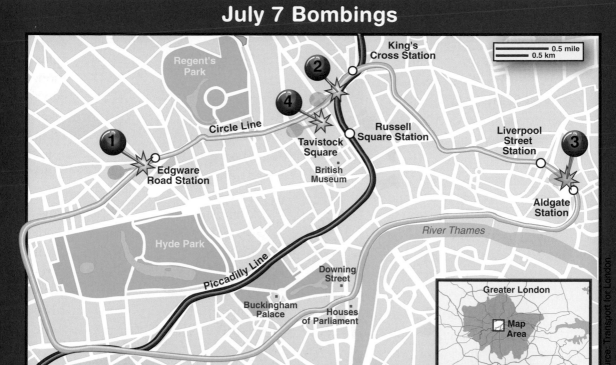

Source: Transport for London.

1 Edgware Road	**2** King's Cross	**3** Aldgate	**4** Tavistock Square
As the train pulls out of Edgware Road station at 8:50 A.M., a bomb blast rips through the second car, leveling a tunnel wall and hitting a nearby train.	At 8:50 A.M. a bomb explodes in the first car of a train traveling deep underground between King's Cross and Russell Square stations.	At 8:50 A.M. a bomb explodes in the third car of a train as it leaves Aldgate station.	At 9:47 A.M. a massive explosion destroys a double-decker bus in Tavistock Square and blasts cars and pedestrians nearby.

choking them. "I remember thinking, 'I'm having a heart attack. A bloody heart attack. This is death. I'm dying and I'm dying on an underground train.'"[12]

"I Hope to God I Will Never See It Again"

Passengers began banging on the windows of the train, trying to break the glass to let in air. "Huge clouds of smoke billowed into the carriage," says one survivor. "It was stinging our eyes and burning our throats. Some were sobbing and others were crying for help. [My friend] Eliot and I stuffed our gym socks in our mouths to stop us choking on the smoke. Someone smashed the windows and outside I could see people covered in cuts stumbling about. There was a man in a suit staggering along the track, clutching his head."[13]

Many of the passengers were unable to flee, especially those who had been in the first car. Twenty-six people were dead, and many others were critically injured. Sergeant Steve

Betts of the British Transport Police, one of the first officers to arrive, was aghast at what he saw as he surveyed the first car. "The entire carriage was just covered head to foot, side to side, in body parts and blood," he says. "The roof had collapsed and fallen inwards and a significant number of bodies were piled up on top of each other on either side of the carriage. I couldn't see how anyone could come out alive. It is the most horrendous and awful scene I have ever seen—and I hope to God I will never see it again."[14]

As Betts walked farther down the track, he heard injured people screaming for help. Many of them were missing limbs. He was most shocked at the sight of a young woman who had neither arms nor legs. "I thought she was dead. I was about to walk on, in search of injured, when she opened her eyes and said, 'Help me.'"[15]

Trying to Calm the Terror

Passengers who had escaped injury or had less severe wounds began helping themselves and others. Some used neckties or belts as tourniquets, helping those around them who were bleeding. Hicks cried for help and hung onto consciousness long enough to tie a scarf around her legs to stanch the flow of blood. She recalls, "I said to myself, 'I am not going

Covering her face with a sterile gauze mask, an injured passenger is led away from the Underground.

to die down here. This is not how it ends, not in a train.'"[16]

Fear was another obstacle that had to be overcome. Many of the survivors who were trying to leave the train were terrified. They were more than 500 yards (457m) from the nearest exit, and it was dark. The high-voltage rails posed another threat. "I knew if we panicked, we'd trip on the—possibly live—tracks, and it would be hopeless," says Rachel.

Rachel tried to ease the tension by making jokes to some of the other passengers. "I remember saying, 'If anyone's boss gives them grief for being late, we know what to say to them, eh, girls?' People laughed and we kept saying, 'Not long, it's the long walk to freedom, nearly there.'"[17]

A Delayed Rescue

The rescue crews were delayed in reaching all three of the Underground bomb sites. Crew chiefs were concerned that the tunnels might collapse. They also feared a second bomb at each site. "It is common," says one explosives expert, "for some bombers to plant a second bomb specifically to impede police or paramedics who are trying to help the victims and otherwise do their jobs."[18]

The three bombs went off within seconds of one another, and at first law enforcement authorities were not sure what had happened. They wondered if there had been a collision between Underground trains or a power surge that caused an explosion. By the time the third blast was reported to authorities, it was clear to those aboveground that something below was very, very wrong.

Injured passengers leave London's Edgware Road station.

At first, the public knew nothing about what had happened. They knew only that the trains were suddenly very slow. Several announcements at Underground stations told commuters that the system was being shut down. Not surprisingly, these announcements caused confusion and annoyance. "Everyone was looking for buses to take them to work or wherever," says London shopkeeper Terry Kirby. "No one was told why—I think people just believed it was a mechanical failure or something, so they didn't have enough information to be anything but put out. Nothing was moving, nothing at all, and people were put out a bit, you know?"[19]

The gridlock made it difficult for emergency crews to respond. Police cars and other responders were stalled in traffic far from the places they were most needed. Within an hour, the Underground was closed. No one was certain whether there might be more bombs, and even if there were not, the tracks in at least three areas were blocked with the debris of the bombed trains.

Without ambulances, rescuers had to improvise. Many of the injured at the Aldgate station were gently put aboard a double-decker bus. When the bus itself became stuck in traffic, a police officer got off and ran a few feet ahead of the bus, shouting at drivers to get out of the way.

A Question, and Then an Explosion

Dozens of police officers worked as traffic controllers, diverting buses and cars from the blast sites. Not only were scores of emergency vehicles trying to get through, but the streets were clogged with thousands of commuters who had been told they would have to find other means of transportation.

Taxis and buses were quickly filled—one of them the No. 30 bus, a red-and-white double-decker driven by forty-nine-year-old George Psaradakis. He was an experienced driver, but the police had diverted him from his normal route, and he found himself in an unfamiliar section of the city near the University of London.

Steven Thornhill happened to be walking near the university at 9:45 A.M. when he saw the crowded bus idling along the side of the road. Just as Thornhill realized the driver must be lost, he heard Psaradakis call out to a nearby police officer, asking where he was. The police officer replied, "Tavistock Square, mate."[20] An instant later, the bus exploded.

"I Thought All My Passengers Were Dead"

When the bomb went off, Psaradakis thought at first he had blown a tire. But when he realized that the roof had blown off the bus, he recalls, "I thought all my passengers were dead."[21]

At that same moment, an American theater producer named Lou Stein heard a loud thud from his apartment about 100 yards (91m) away. He ran outside and was shocked at what he saw. "It was oddly silent," he recalls, "with a lot of distressed people crying into each other's arms. The top of the bus was lifted off, like the top of a tin can that's just been ripped open. There was smoke everywhere."[22]

Thirteen people died in the explosion aboard the No. 30 bus.

Imagining a Suicide Bomber

After the bombings, Londoner Daphna Baram recalled the feelings she had in Jerusalem, where suicide bombings seemed to be an everyday occurrence. The following is an excerpt from her article "Suddenly, Living in London Reminds Me of Being in Jerusalem."

"While Jerusalem was hit by suicide bombers over and over again, London was a virgin to this phenomenon. Not even the IRA bombings of the 1980s could prepare you for the idea that somebody is willing to sacrifice their own life to take yours: it is a difficult idea to come to terms with. Many Londoners wonder what they will do if what everyone hoped was a one-off [a one-time event] turns into a daily reality: how does one live with this type of fear? . . .

I always thought of myself as fearless and, as I told my friends boldly, 'too devoid of imagination to picture it happening to me.' Yet I couldn't but ask myself around 2002 why it was that, after years of slobbiness, I was suddenly leaving the kitchen clean in the mornings and wearing only matching underwear when I went into town. The answers were painfully telling: I didn't want anybody to find piles of dishes in the sink when coming over to clear my belongings, and I wanted even less to be seen on television being carried on a stretcher wearing Bridget Jones knickers that don't even match the bra."

Other witnesses said the scene looked like a war zone, with severed limbs and blood everywhere. The walls of the British Medical Association headquarters, across the street from the ruined bus, were smeared with blood.

Thirteen people were killed in the blast, and many of those who survived were bloody and dazed. One woman, who was in front of the bus when it exploded, says it was the worst experience of her life: "I thought I was going to die. There were people lying on the ground, the bus was belching smoke. . . . Everywhere, people were running, trying to use their mobile phones. It was just mayhem, like World War Three."[23]

"This Was Not Something 'Ordinary'"

Passersby reacted to the crisis immediately. Dr. Andrew Dearden, who was in the British Medical Association building when the bomb went off, heard the noise and believed it to be a collision. "I noticed that the bus was missing its roof and that the back of the bus looked like someone had stepped on it and squashed it down," he says. "I was a bit surprised that I could not see another vehicle near the bus capable of causing that amount of damage that high up the bus— for example, one of these mobile cranes."

As Dearden ran toward the scene, it dawned on him what must have occurred.

"I began to see . . . people's possessions lying around. I saw a lady's purse, I think. Then I ran past a dismembered limb lying on the floor and began to see other parts of human bodies. It was then it hit me that this was not something 'ordinary,' that this was something bad. I know that sounds a bit simple, but it says exactly what I felt."[24]

Other employees of the British Medical Association helped, too. They took apart tables to use as stretchers to move the wounded. They also assisted the medical staff by bringing oxygen, IV hookups, and other needed supplies.

Some of the doctors had never participated in emergency work outside the sterile, controlled environment of an operating room. However, as one doctor at the scene notes, the doctors realized that no matter what their specialty, they must do their best for the victims of the attack. "At first you think, 'Oh, my God,' and then everything slams into gear."[25]

"The Best of Things and the Worst"

Meanwhile, shopkeepers and office workers provided some of the first assistance to survivors emerging from the Underground. At Edgware Road, some of the wounded who straggled into the streets walked into a nearby clothing store. The manager

Injured passengers walk from the scene of one of the bombings to receive treatment for their wounds.

As rescue workers and passersby look on, survivors leave one of the London train stations.

moved merchandise racks aside and found places for them to sit. Some of the staff who knew first aid took clothing from the shelves to use as makeshift bandages and tourniquets. Others ran to snack shops and brought back bottles of water and soda. The concern of people for one another was the only bright spot of the day. As one witness said later, "We saw the best of things and the worst of things."[26]

Chapter Two

"We Shall Prevail"

As soon as government authorities heard reports of explosions on the Underground trains, they notified Prime Minister Tony Blair. Blair was hosting the leaders of eight industrialized nations, called the G8, at a meeting in Scotland. Blair's aides guessed that the the explosions had resulted from a collision or electrical problems. The 142-year-old Underground system frequently experienced electrical malfunctions, and Blair's aides assured him that there was no need for alarm.

"Right Now, We Are All Londoners"

Within an hour, Blair's aides called with information about the true cause of the explosions. It was clear to the arriving G8 leaders that something was wrong as soon as they saw Blair. Normally smiling and congenial, the prime min-

British prime minister Tony Blair speaks about the disaster in London.

ister's despair was evident as he briefed the G8 leaders on the disaster unfolding in London.

Following the London bombings, police in other major cities such as New York tightened security on public transportation.

Summit participants expressed shock at the bombings, and leaders around the world sent messages of outrage and sympathy. The mayor of Paris, who had just hours before learned that London had upstaged his city for the 2012 Olympic games, sent a heartfelt message of condolence. "Right now," said Mayor Bertrand Delanoe, "we are all Londoners."[27]

International Response

Besides offering sympathy and support to the British government, many nations reacted by stepping up their own security.

Though law enforcement authorities could not yet say who had carried out the attacks, many believed al Qaeda, the Muslim extremist group led by Osama bin Laden, was responsible. Al Qaeda had carried out the September 11, 2001, attacks in the United States and the bombing of commuter trains in Madrid in 2004, a catastrophe that killed 191 people. But no matter who was behind the bombings, it seemed critical for other nations to tighten their security, especially in mass transit systems.

France and Italy beefed up security at their ports and borders, as well as on railways and subway networks. France's government announced that those suspected of being affiliated with al Qaeda would be monitored closely. Germany added extra personnel to its transit systems, as well as large shopping plazas and amusement centers.

In the United States, the secretary of homeland security put all mass transit agencies on a heightened alert status. In New York City, thousands of armed police officers patrolled the city's subway system. Signs warned that all backpacks and other large carry-on bags were subject to inspection. Extra security was also placed at the tunnels and bridges that connect the island of Manhattan to the rest of the city. Trains, airport shuttles, and ferry networks were staffed with triple the usual number of security personnel.

London Shut Down

The British government and law enforcement agencies also reacted quickly. Soldiers and the Royal Air Force were put on alert, and police presence in London was tripled, as all personnel were called in to work.

As a precaution against further attacks, the entire London Underground was shut

---

"The Message of the Week"

In her daily postings on the BBC Web site about the bombing of the King's Cross train on which she was a passenger, Rachel [not her real name] looks back on the experience. The excerpt below was posted a week later, on July 14.

"The day began in a crowded carriage, crammed with people, with an act of murderous barbarity. With a bang, smoke, shock, and fear.

Yet almost immediately, even in the choking darkness, in the almost-animal panic, we remembered our humanity, that we were human beings. We stood up, we comforted each other, we held hands, and if we could, we led and carried each other to safety.

The selfish need to claw and fight for survival, to stampede, to free ourselves at all cost did not win; instead, the learned behavior of city dwellers, who must live in close proximity with strangers took over. And that has been the message of the week. We are a civilized society; we live closely and socially in crowded cities. We do not always agree, often we do not talk to each other or look at each other in the face.... But this week we felt what it is like to come together as a city.

To my family, [boyfriend] John and my friends, to my fellow passengers, to my neighbors and fellow citizens in London: I am so glad to be here and I wish us all calmness and hope as we continue with our daily lives.

Crowded together, shoulder to shoulder, I wouldn't have it any other way."

down, as was the city's Heathrow Airport. Aboveground trains and buses heading to London were stopped before they reached the city. The cell phone network was temporarily switched off, too. In the past, some terrorists have used cell phones to detonate bombs, so by shutting down the system, authorities ensured terrorists could not use cell phones in this way. Police closed off streets leading to government buildings, including the Palace of Westminster, where the houses of Parliament meet; Buckingham Palace, where the queen resides; and Blair's residence at 10 Downing Street.

As news of the bombings was broadcast throughout the city, a number of offices and businesses shut down for the day. There was virtually no transportation out of the city, however, and tens of thousands of people packed coffee shops and pubs. "There's nowhere to go," one man told reporters. "I'm watching the [television] coverage here, and I don't know if I'll even get home tonight. There's no train for me to take, so I guess I'm staying here."[28]

"We Will Not Be Intimidated"

As investigative teams joined rescue workers and police at the scenes of the four explosions, the prime minister addressed the people of Britain. Standing next to him as he spoke were French president Jacques Chirac and U.S. president George W. Bush.

"We will not allow violence to change our societies or our values," he said. "Nor will we let it stop the work of this summit. We will continue our deliberations in the interests of a better world. Here at this summit, the world's leaders are striving to combat world poverty and save and improve human life. The perpetrators of today's attacks are intent on destroying life. The terrorists will not succeed. . . . We shall prevail and they shall not."[29]

Blair urged Britons to carry on with their lives and not give in to fear. He reminded his audience that no one yet knew with certainty who was responsible for the attacks, and that the investigation was just beginning. He urged Britons to be strong and brave, even though the events of that day were without a doubt the most frightening in recent years.

Blair said, "When they try to intimidate us, we will not be intimidated. When they seek to change our country or our way of life by these methods, we will not be changed. When they try to divide our people or weaken our resolve, we will not be divided and our resolve will hold firm."[30]

The "Blitz Spirit"

Blair's words recalled a time long ago when the British people faced an even greater threat. During World War II, German warplanes conducted a massive nighttime bombing campaign, known as the Blitz (short for *blitzkrieg*, meaning "lightning war"), against the city. German dictator Adolf Hitler hoped to demoralize and frighten civilians, in hopes of making a German invasion of Britain easier. Sixty thousand people were killed by the bombings, but Britons never gave in to Hitler's terrorist campaign.

Two weeks after the bombings, a municipal worker in London displays a defiant message.

The stoic, defiant attitude demonstrated by Londoners during that frightening time became legendary. Just a few days after the July 7 transit system attacks, a ceremony was held in London commemorating the sixtieth anniversary of the end of World War II. At the ceremony, Queen Elizabeth recalled the bravery of the British people during the Blitz, and urged Britons to show that same "Blitz spirit" again.

"During the present, difficult days for London," she said, "people turn to the example set by that generation—of resilience, humor, sustained courage, often under conditions of great deprivation."[31]

"Life Does Go On"

Just as Americans were urged to continue on with their lives after the attacks against the World Trade Center and the Pentagon on September 11, 2001, many Londoners felt it was their patriotic duty to refuse to give in to fear. "Life does go on," explained one young man two days after the attacks. "This is London, and we can't be beaten by a bunch of bloody thugs. To get on with our lives is a matter of pride."[32]

Just a day after the attacks, commuters returned to London's transit system.

At a public gathering a week after the terrorist attacks, a Union Jack conveys Londoners' refusal to be intimidated.

The same spirit showed itself in a Web site that was created within hours of the attacks. Individual British citizens posted their photos with a simple caption underneath proclaiming, "I Am Not Afraid." In the same vein, a variety of t-shirts were printed and sold in London with bold messages such as "Is that all you've got?" and "Brother, did you pick the wrong city!" One popular shirt carried the logo of the Underground with the words "Not Scared" underneath it.

"I'm Not Brave"

But many Londoners could not get on with their lives, nor could they project a defiant, "Blitz spirit" attitude. Many citizens had been terrorized by the randomness of the attacks and felt unable to carry on life as

31

Remembering 9/11

After the July 7 attack in London, bloggers from around the world sent messages of hope and goodwill to the people of Britain via the Internet. One message, published on the Guardian Unlimited *site, "Your Messages of Support," was from a New York woman who was struck by the similarities to September 11, 2001.*

"I remember 9/11 here in New York City. When I heard [about yesterday's attacks], I thought back to 9/11 and the pain I went through living in Manhattan at that time. London, like New York, is a wonderful, all-inclusive city where people of many races live together in relative harmony. I lived in London for three months several years ago and remember remarking to friends how similar the city was to New York in that it was truly an international place where everyone is accepted for who they are.

Last week on the subway, I met a group of students who came to New York to study this very point . . . to see with their own eyes a city where all people can come together to live and work. These cities are models for the world. I cannot even begin to understand why someone would bring such pain to these places. God or Allah or whatever you choose to call our creator must be wondering right now when we are ever going to understand."

normal in the days immediately following the bombings of July 7.

Trevor, a twenty-four-year-old pub worker, says he tried going to work the following day, but felt nervous. He went home instead and watched CNN coverage of the attacks. His parents suggested that he take a few days off work, and that maybe he would feel more confident after a rest, but he didn't think that would help.

One London businesswoman said she made the decision to leave London for a while. She was riding the Underground system when the bombs went off, although her train was not one of the ones targeted. Even so, she felt fearful and depressed. "I've been breaking down every single day," she said. "Yesterday I walked into the Tube station and broke out in cold sweat and anxiety. I looked at the people around me and I was so amazed at how brave they are. I need some distance. I'm not brave."[33]

Katie McCann, a language teacher in London, says she listened to the speeches by British political leaders urging people to be defiant and brave in the face of terrorism. Their words did not help her feel less fearful. Instead, she says, she has been beset by terrifying thoughts about the September 11 attacks in the United States, and worries that the bombs of July 7 are just the beginning. She even worries that hijacked jets will crash into her apartment complex.

McCann says that references to World War II and how Londoners coped with the Blitz do not seem to her to be relevant today. "I feel that they're out of touch," she says. "There is no community. We are all alone here."[34]

Waiting for the Phone to Ring

Family and friends of the missing, injured, and dead probably experienced the most difficulty. The recovery of bodies was exceedingly slow, especially on the train deep in the tunnel below King's Cross station. In addition, because of the violent nature of the attacks, many of the victims' bodies were unrecognizable. Identification of bodies moved very slowly as well, and forensic workers announced that it might be days or weeks before they would be able to say exactly who had been killed.

Many people put up photographs and signs asking for assistance in locating missing friends or family members. Posters asking "Have You Seen This Person?" were plastered over walls and buildings near King's Cross station as well as in Tavistock

In the days following the bombings, friends and relatives of those still missing posted appeals for help in locating their loved ones.

Square, where the No. 30 bus was bombed. These two sites had the most casualties, and the most people missing.

Photographs of the missing showed a wide range of people—a smiling woman in graduation robes, a man proudly holding his new baby, a grandmother waving at the camera. They were immigrants, native Britons, and tourists. There was nothing uniform about them, except that they were missing—and that their families and friends were anxiously hoping for a phone call indicating they had somehow survived.

"I've Cried a Lot"

In the days immediately after the attacks, many Londoners were desperate for word of missing loved ones. One frantic father worried over the fate of his daughter Miriam, a photographer. He was certain she was not on any of the bombed trains, but he was not sure whether she might have taken a bus. "I haven't got a plausible explanation," he said sadly. "She is the kind of person that if she was not going to get home in the evening, she would have told us and phoned home."[35]

Another man said he was optimistic that someone would spot his girlfriend because of her spiky blonde haircut. "I've cried a lot," he told reporters. "It's so up and down. . . . But her hair would stand out." He said he was frustrated when he called the police because they were unable to tell him anything. "I called them three times," he said, "and they said they have nothing new. I told them I would continue to call until I was blue in the face."[36]

Another man was overwhelmed with the idea that his girlfriend, a young woman from Israel, might have been killed in the explosion on the No. 30 bus. He was talking to her on her cell phone while she was riding on the bus, and heard the blast. He heard screaming, and then the line went dead. "The irony of all these terrible things," he said, "is that she was afraid of going back to Israel because she was scared of suicide bombings on the buses."[37]

"This Is Absolutely Appalling"

For some of those awaiting word about loved ones, frustration and grief turned to anger at authorities over the slow pace of identification of the victims. For days, families walked through hospital emergency areas and makeshift morgues near the blast sites several times each day. "This is absolutely appalling," said one man, distraught over his missing fiancée. "A Third World country would do a better job of it."[38]

Another man, awaiting word of an American friend on the No. 30 bus, understood the feelings of frustration, but said he realized that the bodies were part of an investigation. The retrieval of bodies—and parts of bodies—was a difficult, time-consuming job. "We're all frustrated how slow it is to identify the victims, whether dead or alive, of this kind of disaster. But we want to make it clear that we are not frustrated with the authorities. We don't feel they are lagging." He said that the delay for families was just another excruciating aspect of the bombings: "We're playing a waiting game, which is awful."[39]

Londoners turned to one another for comfort in the aftermath of the bombings.

Two tourists read a British tabloid's account of the bombings that had occurred earlier that day.

Another Kind of Worry

A wait of a different sort went on in London's downtown business district. Business owners worried what effects the terrorist attacks would have on their livelihood. In the days after the attacks, many businesses had far fewer customers than usual.

"The lunchtime trade is definitely down," observed one restaurant manager, "because people are avoiding midday travel. And in the evenings I've noticed that people are going out less. I think that much like [after the attacks in New York] on 9/11, this has left people feeling more family-oriented, wanting to stay in more and be with loved ones."[40]

Tourism is a key part of the economy of Britain, especially during the summer months. Immediately after the bombings, large numbers of tourists scrambled to escape London. Airlines had to add extra flights to accommodate the people who wanted to leave. Those who had already booked trips to Britain were nervous, too. Many called travel agencies wanting to change their plans—either canceling or postponing their trips to a later time, when it might be safer.

"I hope things settle down," one hotel desk attendant said several days after the bombings. He had taken several calls that morning—all of them cancellations. "It's bad for business—bad for everyone. We're hoping that in a few days things will sort themselves out and we can get busy, as we're used to this time of year."[41]

A Roller Coaster of Emotions

Of all the various reactions to the bombings, the most wide ranging and compelling were those of the hundreds of people who survived. No matter what the extent of their injuries—or whether they were injured at all—the bombings created a roller coaster of emotions.

One passenger on the No. 30 bus, who sustained shrapnel wounds to her legs, said that even after three months she continued to experience flashbacks to the bombing. Loud noises gave her the most trouble. "I was walking down the street and someone dropped a bottle," she explained. "There was a loud smash and then all this broken glass and I started to panic. . . . I feel like my life has been put on hold."[42]

Victims experienced other reactions, too. A man who had been on the Edgware train told reporters that the experience made him want to stay home with his wife and children and never leave again. A young woman who had been on the Aldgate train experienced nausea and dizziness when she heard the sound of an approaching train. Another survivor of the same train blast said he was unable to sleep more than twenty minutes at a time. He dreamed about the bombing and woke in a cold sweat.

One London woman who has survived suicide bombings in Israel says that the range of feelings is universal to survivors of such violence: "I have a friend who used to get surges of panic while sitting in a cafe and run out, leaving his coffee undrunk and the bill unpaid. Another used to make bus drivers let her off intercity buses in the middle of nowhere, shivering with panic."[43]

Too Much Pluck

Some survivors admitted they felt guilty that they could not respond with the defiance and stoicism for which Londoners were known. One said she was almost giddy after the bombings, when she had been bandaged up by triage doctors near the Aldgate station. She even wanted to go to work, to see her friends and show them she was fine. But the next day, she was too terrified to get out of bed.

Experts in traumatic stress say that comparisons to the events of World War II are not helpful. The two events are not the same. Putting up a strong front in this case can disguise feelings that a victim may need to deal with in order to heal. It is crucial for victims of the London bombings not to feel that they have to live up to anyone else's standards of bravery. "There is a resilience around, a kind of intent not to let the bombers triumph," one counselor says. But the outward pluck tends to hide the suffering within, and that can create other problems. "A lot of people need to be very gentle with themselves right now."[44]

Rachel, a young woman who survived the King's Cross bombing, forced herself to return to work the Tuesday following the blast. This gave her no time to deal with her bouts of fear, guilt over having survived when others had not, and uncontrollable weeping. Although her physical wounds had healed, her emotional wounds were still raw, as she quickly discovered when she got to work. "I arrived something of a nervous wreck," she says. "It was very hard to focus. Twice I had to hide in the [bathroom] and have a quick weep for ten minutes."[45]

A Moment of Silence

One of the most meaningful attempts at dealing with the grief and sadness on a citywide level occurred a week after the bombings, on July 14. It was a two-minute period of silence to honor those who had died in the attacks.

Beginning exactly at noon, airports, train stations, stores, factories, schools, and universities fell silent. Though the trains continued to run, the passengers were silent, and Underground staff wore black armbands. One newspaper reporter described the scene in her office and on the street below as noon approached:

> Just before midday today, a steadily growing stream of *Guardian* staff trooped silently down the five flights of stairs from our offices onto Farringdon Road, normally one of London's busier streets. A crowd gathered in front of the building, matched by similar silent gatherings all along the road. A double decker bus, a No. 63, pulled over and switched off its engine. The driver stepped outside his cab and his passengers rose from their seats . . . [and] for two brief minutes . . . this small corner of London paid its respects to the people who died in last Thursday's attacks on our city.[46]

Rachel noted in her diary that the silence and the memorial service that evening were helpful to her own healing

A week after the bombings, Londoners gathered in Trafalgar Square for a memorial vigil.

process. She said that it felt good to be with other Londoners, all feeling many of the same emotions. "Now we need to remember what this sense of unity feels like," she wrote. "We will need to remember it in the difficult weeks and months ahead."[47]

Chapter Three

Investigating Four Bombings

While the people of London were dealing with the emotional and physical toll of the bombings, the city's Metropolitan Police were beginning their investigation. Investigators knew that speed was crucial not only to bring the terrorists to justice, but also to prevent more bombings—a scenario experts felt was quite likely. As one police official noted, "We can't possibly assume that what happened on Thursday [July 7] was the last of these events."[48]

The Largest Investigation in History

The investigation of the July 7 transit system bombings was the largest criminal investigation in Britain's history. The entire Metropolitan Police force was assigned to the case, along with four hundred officers of London's antiter-rorist branch and some Special Branch investigators, who had a great deal of training in bombing cases.

Britain also had help from countries worldwide. The United States and more than twenty European nations sent detectives and forensic specialists to London to work with the Metropolitan Police. The FBI doubled the number of agents at its field office in London and offered the use of its crime laboratories.

Police officials told the public that the investigation would likely be a long one. Any bombing is a difficult crime to solve, simply because the bomb itself is blown apart into millions of tiny pieces. Forensic specialists processing a bombing scene know that it is a difficult, painstaking job that sometimes yields very few clues.

The London bombings took place at four different sites, so even more

Forensic investigators comb the wreckage of the No. 30 bus in search of evidence.

time and labor would be needed to process the scenes. "Often there is no real golden nugget, no piece of evidence that brings it all together," explains a former FBI agent. "You're talking about fragments that are scattered over different crime scenes—a seemingly endless stream of evidence."[49]

Every Detail Is Important

The investigators began by barricading each crime scene. In the case of the three Underground sites, those sections of track were shut down completely. The bus was surrounded with large screens of plastic sheeting, and that part of Tavistock Square was blocked off for a few days while crews processed the vehicle and debris on site.

The intent of the investigation was to find out who was responsible for the bombings—even if the bombers themselves had died in the explosion. The most important clues to the identities of those responsible would be in the bombs themselves—the type of explosive used, the way the timers and detonators were constructed, and even the method used to wire them. Several high-profile bombing cases in the United States had previously been solved just by the type of duct tape and wire used by the bombers. "You say to your-

This train and the other bombing sites were examined in minute detail for clues to the identity of those responsible.

self, what details about the construction [of a bomb] are important," says one explosives expert. "And the answer is 'Everything.'"[50]

Finding the parts of a bomb—or, in this case, four bombs—is a study in patience. Investigators find the seat, or origin, of the explosion, by looking at the patterns of scorching and heat damage at the site. The more damage to seats, metal fixtures, and even the bodies themselves, the closer they likely were to the bomb. Once the seat of the explosion has been located, investigators and forensic crews fan out from that point, looking for fragments of the bomb embedded in the surrounding area and debris.

"We Have Got to Get This Right"

Part of the surrounding area includes the bodies of the victims. After the rescue crews make certain that all survivors have been helped away from the scene, removing the bodies is not a priority. At every fatal bombing scene, the bodies of the dead are considered part of the crime scene, and are processed as such.

Although it was a source of anger and frustration for the families and friends of the missing—and presumed dead—at the four London bombing scenes, it was vital to the investigation that the bodies be

Forensic investigators examine the façade of a building at Tavistock Square in search of evidence in the No. 30 bus bombing.

processed before they were released for burial. The bodies would be swabbed for explosive residue and X-rayed to see whether they contained bits of the bomb.

Identification of the bodies was a vital part of the investigation for another reason. If the attacks had been carried out by suicide bombers, their bodies would be at

Bomb Blast near King's Cross Station

The bomb exploded in the first car of a train traveling in a narrow tunnel deep underground. The explosion shattered windows, twisted metal, and blew a hole in the floor of the train. Survivors who could walk endured fumes, rats, smoke, and 140 degree heat as they struggled toward the nearest exit, about a half mile away. Others had to wait many hours for rescuers to pull them out of the rubble.

60 feet below ground

Source: *Newsweek*, July 18, 2005.

the scene as well as those of the victims. Identifying all bodies as well as matching body parts to torsos, and so on, would be difficult because the explosions were so violent. Because it was impossible to visually identify most of the victims, forensic workers had to rely on DNA testing, dental records, and fingerprints, all of which took time.

Ian Blair, commissioner of the Metropolitan Police, apologized for the slow pace, but begged for patience. "I appeal to everybody to give us time," he said at a news conference three days after the bombings. "We have got to get this right."[51]

"A Tunnel of Blood"

The processing and recovery of the dead was most difficult at King's Cross station. The bomb had gone off after the train descended into a tunnel that is more than 60 feet (20m) underground. The tunnel itself was built more than one hundred years ago, when builders bored through the rock and clay, and reinforced it with large iron rings. It is very narrow, with only a few inches' clearance on either side of the train. The narrowness of the tunnel made the damage to the train and its passengers far worse than at the other train bombing sites. *New York Times* reporter Craig Smith wrote that the bomb sent its force "punching through the cars like a blast down the barrel of a shotgun."[52]

The bombed train had been traveling from King's Cross station to Russell Square when the explosion occurred. Because of the extensive damage on the King's Cross

end of the tunnel, recovery crews were forced to travel to the bombing site from Russell Square, one-third of a mile away. Battery-operated trolleys shuttled in crews, investigators, and equipment, and brought out human remains as they were processed.

Dozens of recovery workers came to London from all over the world. However, because of the cramped conditions at King's Cross, only a few workers at a time could get to the site. The recovery teams, dressed in white protective suits, had to crawl carefully in single file into the tunnel, inches at a time, so as not to disturb evidence.

After four days, recovery teams had taken out all visible remains. However, they acknowledged the possibility that there were still bodies they could not get to underneath the train—bodies that might have been blown out through the front of the train and subsequently run over.

"Things You Would Not Wish Anyone to See"

Investigators who had worked at other bombing sites through the years were appalled by the conditions below King's Cross. One police officer called it "a tunnel of blood."[53] Ian Blair stated that working at King's Cross was "a job of extraordinary horror."[54]

Not only was there a great deal of human carnage, but the conditions under which recovery teams worked were extremely unpleasant. The temperature in the tunnel

Shrouded in protective plastic, one of the wrecked train cars is lifted by crane onto a nearby flatbed truck. It will be transported to a secure site for further forensic examination.

topped 120°F (49°C), the generator, lights, and lingering heat from the bomb itself made it even hotter. In addition, workers battled aggressive rats, lured to the site by the smell of the bodies.

Trauma teams came to the area to provide counseling for the workers, some of whom were crying as they came aboveground each day. "Many of the firemen and police were very young," says one priest, who offered his services as a counselor to some of the teams. "It was their first experience with something so horrific. They went down with an amazing sense of courage and came up having seen things you would not wish anyone to see."[55]

An Internet Claim

As forensic teams were doing their work, other investigators were puzzling over a claim of responsibility for the bombings that appeared on a radical Islamic Web site soon after the explosions. The posting, from a group calling itself the Secret Organization Group of al Qaeda of Jihad Organization, said that the group was behind all four of the bombings. The British media released the statement, which had been translated from Arabic.

The statement said that the attacks were revenge against the British government for its role in the war on terror being fought in Iraq and Afghanistan. Since Britain was the staunchest ally of the United States, the group believed the nation deserved to be the target of what it called "a blessed attack in London." The posting hinted that the bombings had struck fear into people in every part of London. Because of the bombs on the transit system, the posting claimed, Britain was "burning now out of fear in its north, south, east, and west."[56] Some authorities

The Shoe Bomber

When it was discovered that the explosive TATP had been used in the July 7 bombings, investigators were reminded of another British would-be terrorist with an al Qaeda link. On December 22, 2001—just weeks after the attacks of September 11 in the United States—a British Muslim named Richard Reid was arrested after trying to blow up an American Airlines jet on which he was a passenger. The airliner was traveling from Paris to Miami.

A flight attendant smelled smoke, as though a match had been lit, and went to investigate. She found Reid trying to ignite a substance inside the tongue of his tennis shoe. She tried to grab the shoe from his hand, but he pushed her to the floor and continued trying to set his shoe on fire. Passengers tackled Reid and held him until the plane could land. Antiterrorism investigators found that Reid's shoe contained enough TATP to blow up the plane and kill everyone aboard.

Reid stated that he was in league with Osama bin Laden, the mastermind of the September 11 attacks. The Shoe Bomber, as Reid became known, was found guilty of three separate charges related to the incident in January 2003 and sentenced to life in prison.

The London transit system bombs contained TATP, the same explosive Richard Reid (above) used in his failed attempt to blow up a jetliner several years earlier.

interpreted this as meaning that the transit systems in all four sections of the city had been interrupted by the attacks.

The claim on the Internet was interesting, but investigators had never heard of this particular group. False claims are not uncommon after terrorist acts. It was entirely possible that this group was an offshoot of the larger al Qaeda organization, but until investigators had more information, they could not say whether the claim was authentic. "We will be looking into [the Internet claim] as well as any other leads," said one senior London police official, "but at the moment we don't know if that's a genuine claim or not."[57]

Similarities to al Qaeda Attacks

There were other indicators that the attacks could have been the work of al Qaeda, or perhaps of a group inspired by that terrorist organization. The London bombings bore some key similarities to the 2004 bombing of commuter trains in Madrid,

The London bombings bore many similarities to those that killed 191 passengers aboard commuter trains in Madrid in March 2004.

Spain, which authorities had confirmed were carried out by al Qaeda. For one thing, the targets were the same—the key mass transit system in each country. Also, the attacks were carried out at the height of rush hour in order to kill or injure as many people as possible.

Another similarity was the lack of warning. Many terrorist groups, including the Irish Republican Army (IRA), the source of previous attacks in Britain, have traditionally called in warnings to authorities before setting off a bomb. Al Qaeda has never provided warnings before an attack.

Several intelligence officials from Europe, the United States, and Britain felt that the attacks of July 7 were the work of a group allied with al Qaeda because the radical Islamic group had threatened more attacks like the one in Madrid. "The attack methodology is consistent with what we know al-Qaeda has planned for in the past," said one senior U.S. intelligence agent. "There is also intelligence indicating that al-Qaeda has been trying to carry out attacks in Europe and the [United States] just like this one."[58]

"The Mother of Satan"

The first forensic evidence that pointed to al Qaeda was the residue on the swabs taken from the trains, the bus, and the bodies. Tests on the residue confirmed the presence of the explosive triacetone triperoxide, or TATP. This substance is the explosive of choice for many suicide bombers in Israel, including operatives of al Qaeda.

The presence of TATP at the four bombing scenes indicated to investigators that there was a very good chance that the bombers were extremist Muslims, perhaps affiliated with al Qaeda.

TATP is usually concocted from a variety of ingredients, including drain cleaner and hydrogen peroxide, that can be purchased almost anywhere without raising suspicion. It is also a very powerful homemade explosive, so unstable and combustible that it is often accidentally detonated as it is being made. In a period of less than three years, as many as forty potential suicide bombers are known to have been killed in making batches of TATP. It is not hard to understand why it has been nicknamed "the Mother of Satan."

A Gruesome Clue

Because TATP is so often associated with suicide bombers, investigators of the London bombing began to focus on the condition of the bodies of victims at each of the bombing scenes. Israeli investigators, who have a great deal of experience with suicide bombers, know that someone carrying a bomb—either in a pack or strapped to his or her chest, as suicide bombers in the Middle East often do—suffers a great amount of damage to the skin and organs within the torso. The bomber's head and arms are often blown off, but these extremities usually lack gashes or other wounds. While people near the bomber may also lose arms and legs in the explosion, there are noticeable burns and other damage to those limbs.

Investigators at the site of the No. 30 bus at Tavistock Square had found a body with its head ripped cleanly off. Although the body's condition was not ironclad evidence that it was that of the bomber, it was the best lead they had thus far. The lead seemed even more promising when investigators received a frantic call from a woman in Leeds, a city about 200 miles (320km) north of London.

The woman said her eighteen-year-old son, Hasib Hussain, had been missing for days. She said he had mentioned that he might be going to London with some friends, but she had not heard from him and worried he might have been on one of the bombed trains or the bus. She provided a photograph of her son and gave names and descriptions of some of his friends.

Her description of her son matched the remains of the suspected bomber on the bus, and identification found inside the clothing on the body showed that the man was Hasib Hussain. Even more promising to the investigation, police were able to match the names of Hussain's friends to the names on credit cards and other papers found at the three Underground bombing sites.

"He Was Standing Next to Me"

Eyewitness statements made by some of the passengers on the No. 30 bus also proved helpful. A sixty-one-year-old businessman named Richard Jones had a good look at the person he believed was the bomber, whom he described as a young, handsome, olive-skinned man who had a knapsack with him.

Jones says the man had seemed nervous and agitated.

"He was standing next to me with the bag at his feet," Jones recalls, "and he kept dipping into this bag and fiddling about with something. I was getting quite annoyed, because this was a crowded bus. You can imagine the crush—it was standing room only. Everybody is standing face to face, and this guy kept dipping into his bag."[59]

Jones's description fit Hussain, and police had a theory about what he had been doing with his knapsack. "We now assume he was adjusting a timer or something on the bomb itself," one investigator explained to news reporters. "He was nervous about it, according to witnesses, maybe because it was set to go off at a later point, and since there were delays [because the Underground had been shut down after the three bombings] . . . the timing was off, or something. We can only speculate now, but that seems a likely explanation."[60]

Using London's Mechanical Eyes

In hopes of identifying all the bombers, investigators turned to the thousands of closed-circuit television (CCTV) cameras that monitor the city of London. The cameras, which were installed to help protect the city against IRA bombings, are virtually everywhere—stores, restaurants, street corners, buses, and Underground stations. There are so many, in fact, that experts estimate the average Londoner is photographed between thirty and forty times each day.

Forensic investigators remove a body from the scene of the No. 30 bus bombing.

There are more than six thousand CCTV cameras in the London transportation system, so there was a good chance that the image of at least one of the bombers would appear on some of the videotapes. The task of reviewing so many hours of tape in hopes of catching a glimpse of one of the bombers was daunting, however. One police source acknowledged, "It is a massive job that is very time consuming."[61]

Hundreds of extra officers were deployed just to go through thousands of hours of tape—not only from each train, but from each of the cameras outside the forty train stations on the Underground routes, as well as the cameras in the areas where passengers boarded the No. 30 bus. It was the largest CCTV recovery the Metropolitan Police Department had ever participated in. "We are working at it day and night," said one investigator. "Twenty-four hours, round the clock. We've no room for mistakes here, so everyone is very keyed into their task."[62]

Catching the Bombers on Camera

The search of the CCTV videotapes intensified after police distributed copies of Hussain's photograph. Within hours, police spotted him on one of the tapes, taken at King's Cross station at 8:20 A.M. the day of the bombing.

On the tape Hussain was talking with three other men who fit the descriptions provided by Hussain's mother. The conversation ended quickly, and each man went in a different direction. Police viewing the footage were struck by how happy and relaxed the four young men looked. "You would think," said one police official, "they were going on a hiking holiday."[63] Twenty minutes later the three Underground bombs detonated, and three of the men died instantly in the explosions.

Investigators continued to search the tapes, working backward from King's Cross to see the route each man took to get to that station. They found that the men had met twenty-eight miles north of London in a town called Luton, where they caught a train

to King's Cross. Police seized a rental car left by the men at a parking lot in Luton, and found traces of TATP in the car. Other investigators went to the homes of the four men, searching for more evidence. In one apartment they found the bathtub in which the explosives had been mixed, as well as bomb-making chemicals.

"He Was a Nice Bloke"

Though investigators were rapidly learning more about the bombing suspects, what they learned was discouraging. The four young men were not on any terrorist watch lists around the world. Unlike the hijackers responsible for the attacks in the United States on September 11, 2001, none of whom were U.S. citizens, the four London bombers were all British citizens.

Intelligence officials use the term "clean skins" to describe such people. Clean skins have no record of terrorism or other

Cameras such as these mounted near a passenger platform recorded the suspected bombers boarding the trains.

extremism, and thus are able to go about their business unwatched and unsuspected. The four London bombers appeared to be not only clean skins but well-liked and involved in their communities. Hussain, for example, was known as having a great sense of humor, though not much of a student. Nineteen-year-old Germaine Lindsay, identified as the bomber of the King's Cross train, had a young son and always seemed friendly to his neighbors.

Mohammed Sidique Khan, responsible for the Edgware Road train explosion, was married and had a young daughter. He taught at a nearby elementary school and was especially good at helping children with learning problems. "He was a nice bloke," says the father of one of Khan's pupils. "He helped [my nine-year-old son] Joe catch up after he missed six months of school."[64] Shahzad Tanweer, who bombed the Aldgate train, hoped to have a future as a professional soccer player. One of his teammates said there was no indication Tanweer was capable of such a crime, saying simply, "He was normal."[65]

"Exactly What Nobody Wanted to Hear in This Case"

Investigators were discouraged by the realization that the bombers were not foreign

In this image recorded by a CCTV camera on the morning of July 7, the bombers arrive at a station to catch a train bound for London.

Have You Seen Her?

Twenty-four-year-old Carrie Taylor was a passenger on the Aldgate train. Overwhelmed with grief, her mother told *Daily Mail* reporter Charlotte Gill that one of the only comforts she had was that in her last glimpse of her daughter she was smiling and waving goodbye to her.

"Carrie and I travel to Liverpool Street together every day," she said. "I know it sounds silly, but we have a little farewell ritual. As we come through the barriers, she gives me a kiss goodbye before we go our separate ways. Then I watch her as she heads off for the Tube. I always watch until she's out of sight before I make a move. It's a funny little mum's habit, but I'm so

very glad that the last picture I have of her in my head is smiling and waving at me."

Her mother said she was glad, too, that Carrie lived to see London chosen to host the 2012 Olympics. "Carrie was thrilled when she heard London had won. She loved the fact that because she lived in London she was going to live through all the preparations over the next seven years."

At the time the news of the Olympics was announced, her father was redecorating the kitchen. Carrie wrote, "Carrie Louise Taylor 6/7/05—We got the Olympic bid 2012 this day" on the wall her father was about to paint. "I haven't got the heart to wallpaper over her words," her mother said.

terrorists, but instead were British citizens. The unremarkable profiles of the bombers meant there was almost nothing that could have been done by terrorist experts to prevent such attacks—and that further attacks could occur without warning, as well.

"It's exactly what nobody wanted to hear in this case," said one British security expert. "These are normal people from normal lives who, as far as we know, woke up one morning and decided to blow up an Underground train."

He also said that the presence of such people in Britain was alarming, and did not bode well for the future: "That means not only that we didn't know about them, but that we couldn't have—at least before

they acted. It means Londoners are going to have to get used to suicide bombings as a part of life."[66]

Frightening Predictions

Although the investigation had yielded the names of the four bombers quite quickly, other disturbing questions needed to be addressed. Most authorities strongly believed that the four terrorists did not act alone. Said one FBI investigator assisting on the case, "There's a whole other set of individuals that either assembled the devices, set up the residences where they were built, delivered them, or paid for the operation."[67]

A young man looks on while police raid a neighborhood in Leeds, a city north of London where the bombers were thought to have lived.

If this is true, Londoners asked themselves, who are those people? They wondered whether Osama bin Laden was behind the attacks, just as he had been behind the 9/11 attacks in the United States. They wondered, too, whether the associates of the suicide bombers had fled, or if they were still in London. Intelligence sources were not optimistic about the the future, predicting that there would almost certainly be further attacks in London. British intelligence analysts informed the prime minister that there were certainly other terrorist cells in London and the surrounding area, and that it was only a matter of time until the next attack.

Chapter Four

More Violence in the City

After the bombings of July 7, Londoners experienced both shock and fear. Sometimes these feelings came out as aggression and hostility. Even before investigators verified that the bombers were extremist Muslims—most probably affiliated with al Qaeda—the Muslim community in London felt a violent backlash. "Some people just felt powerless," says one London teenager. "They didn't have anyone specific to blame, and they just lashed out at any Muslim who was nearby."[68]

"Get These People Out of Our Country"

The day of the bombing, a mosque was set on fire in Leeds. Police also took many calls from Muslim residents in London reporting that they had been threatened or their property vandalized.

On the Internet thousands of people posted messages of frustration and anger, many aimed at London's Muslim community. "Get these [Muslims] out of our country," wrote one. "I know it isn't all of them, but please, they are ruining our beautiful city, and have no right. I am disgusted—get them out!"[69]

The Internet was also used to spread rumors about Muslim involvement in the bombings. One frequently repeated post informed readers that the Muslim community knew the bombings would occur on July 7, and as a result, London Muslims knew not to ride either the bus or Underground that morning. (Two Muslims actually did die in the attacks.)

Another popular rumor was that throughout the city, Muslims were seen celebrating when word of the attacks came. "A family friend of mine

A police officer directs a Muslim family to safety as a house in their neighborhood in the city of Birmingham is searched as part of the bombing investigation.

witnessed some Muslims in a local Mc-Donald's, clapping and laughing as the London bombing was on the TV!" said another posting. "Why are they in our country?"[70]

"I Am Too Scared Now"

The announcement by investigators that the bombers appeared to have been Muslim extremists only increased the violence and hostility directed at London's Muslim population.

Faith-hate crimes (those committed because of a victim's religion) rose 600 percent in the days after the announcement. Authorities had reports of restaurant owners visited by people threatening to burn down their businesses, of young Muslim men beaten, and even of an Iraqi schoolgirl attacked in a park near her home.

According to the Monitoring Group, a nonprofit organization in London that offers support to victims of racism or other discrimination, hate crimes against elderly Muslims increased, too. One sixty-seven-year-old woman, for example, had never experienced any trouble with neighbors. After the attacks, however, someone threw bricks through her front window, put dog feces on her porch, painted a swastika on her doorway, and vandalized her car. She no longer goes out much, she says, except to visit the mosque every so often. "I am too scared now," she says. "I have no life."[71]

Attackers lashed out at anyone who looked as though they might be from an Asian or Middle Eastern country. "We have had calls from South Americans, eastern Europeans, Hindus, and Sikhs," says a Monitoring Group official. "Ten to 15 percent are people who are a different religion than Muslim. We have one very serious case of a disabled Hindu man who was beaten up by his neighbor and left with severe head injuries, while being called al-Qaeda."[72]

"We Can Die in the Same Bomb"

Many Muslims were hoping the bombers would turn out not to be Muslim. One Iraqi refugee said that she could not bear the

Along with thousands of other Muslim residents, these women living in the city of Leeds attended a memorial rally for victims a week after the transit system bombings.

thought of how white Londoners would act. "I worry about everyone, how our life will be, if al-Qaeda did it," she said. "I'm so afraid. I'm so afraid."[73]

Another woman insisted that Muslims should be clear about showing their sympathy for the British people. A friend quickly corrected her, saying, "We are the British people."[74]

Many Muslims in the neighborhood where some of the suspects lived said that things would be especially difficult for them if the suspects turned out to be guilty of the crimes. They already experienced religious intolerance from people who lived nearby. The bombings, they said, would only make things worse. People would believe that the entire neighborhood was filled with extremists.

"Whether it is one of the lads [who was on the video with Hussain] or none of them," said one young mother, "we all have to suffer. If these people are responsible, then I am scared of getting on a bus myself, because they live round the corner. . . . This is as much a shock to me as it is to a non-Muslim. We live in this country and we can die in the same bomb."[75]

Many Muslim women who wear the traditional hijab headscarves feared they would be easily recognized targets for abuse. Dr. Zaki Badawi, head of the Muslim College in London, publicly urged women to stop wearing the hijab. "In the present, tense situation we advise Muslim women who fear being attacked physically or verbally to remove their hijab so as not to be identified by those hostile to Mus-

lims," he said. "Dress is meant to protect from harm, not to invite it. The preservation of life and limb has a much higher priority than appearance."[76]

"It Makes Me Feel Guilty, and I Shouldn't"

For Muslim teens living in the area where the bombing suspects lived, the time after the bombings was especially hard. Most of them had tried to establish an identity as typical British teenagers while at the same time showing pride in their heritage and religion.

"I go to mosque every day," said one sixteen-year-old boy wearing Nikes and speaking with a broad Yorkshire accent, "but that's my own choice, it's nothing to do with my parents. Racism was a bit of a problem [here] in Leeds, but not that bad, but there's definitely been more towards us . . . since the bombings. When I've been walking in town, people have said stuff like, 'Have you bombed anyone recently?' and worse. I don't know why, but it makes me feel guilty and I shouldn't, because the guys who set off the bombs in London weren't real Muslims."

He admitted to feeling a little nervous walking through his neighborhood after the attacks. "The other day a group of white guys who were drunk threw a bottle at me and called me a bomber," he said, "but the racism only makes my religion stronger."[77]

His friend agreed. "My mum was shouted at when she was going to the

Muslim residents of Leeds, located 200 miles north of London, rally to show their opposition to extremist violence.

butcher's," he said. "They only do it because they want you to react and say something. I ignore them because that's what they don't want you to do."[78]

Trying to Calm the Anger and Fear

Hoping to stem not only the outbreak of racist and religious hate crimes, but also the fear and distrust many Londoners felt toward Muslims, the British government called a meeting of the city's religious leaders three days after the bombings. Influential Christian, Muslim, and Jewish leaders in London

met with Blair, and together they stressed that there must be a distinction between Islam as a religion and the political label of "terrorist."

"Anyone claiming to commit a crime in the name of religion does not necessarily justify his position in the name of that religion," said one Muslim leader. "People do things in the name of Islam which are totally contrary to Islam."[79]

A Christian leader in London urged the public to keep in mind that most of London's 1.8 million Muslims were law-abiding citizens who would never support terrorism. "We all know that the vast majority of our

"The World's Great Powers Are Against Muslims"

In a Minneapolis Star Tribune *article titled "Wrestling with the Enemy Within," Sharon Schmickle interviews a Muslim father who is understandably nervous about the mood in London after the bombings, and concerned about how the climate of distrust will affect him and his family.*

"Across [London] in Southhall, Mohammad Kalim, a 41-year-old electrical engineer, stopped on his way into a mosque to talk about the mixed emotions that tear at him.

'I'm nervous,' Kalim said. 'I like to do photography, but I've stopped carrying my camera bag for fear it will draw suspicion on me.'

He also feels very helpless and conflicted: 'I'm very strongly against extremism, and I wish I could do something to cool it down. That isn't simple. I can stand outside the mosque and make a voice, but there is so much anger, such a strong feeling that the world's great powers are against Muslims . . . I feel angry, as well.'

He also worries about his nine-year-old son: 'I am a very moderate Muslim and I tell him that even when the extremists have the right cause, they have the wrong way of doing it. . . . I hope he doesn't get into bad hands where he doesn't talk to us as a teenager and he talks to the wrong people instead.'"

Muslim friends and neighbors are as horrified and disgusted at what happened as we are," he said. "This will only make us more determined to live in peace and respect each other."[80]

"Go to Another Country— Get Out"

Not all of Britain's leaders were effective in calming the rising emotions throughout London. Tory party spokesman Gerald Howarth sparked a great deal of controversy by suggesting that any Muslims who had extremist beliefs should leave the country.

"There can be no compromise with these people," he said in a newspaper interview. "If they don't like our way of life, there is a simple remedy—go to another country, get out." Asked what he would say to Muslims who were born in Britain, Howarth said it made no difference. "Tough," he snapped. "If you don't give allegiance to this country, then leave. There are plenty of other countries whose way of life would appear to be more conducive to what they aspire to. They would be happy and we would be happy."[81]

Such comments prompted an outcry from moderate Muslim leaders such as Anas Altikriti of the Muslim Association of Britain, who said that Howarth and others were making a bad situation even worse. "Mr. Howarth must realize," Altikriti protested, "that his own statement will have a real and serious bearing on the street. There are people who will take his words and understand them in a particular way and this will induce further harm rather than good."[82]

Another Day of Bombings

On July 21—exactly two weeks after the attacks that killed fifty-six people—a second wave of bombings occurred in London. As before, four bombs targeted the city's mass transit system. Three were on Underground trains—near Oval station, Warren Street, and Shepherd's Bush—and the fourth was on a No. 26 bus in London's East End.

Just as on July 7, the bombers carried explosives in backpacks. But though there were striking similiarities in the organization of the attacks, the damage done by the July 21 bombings was minimal. There were no deaths, and the only injuries appear to have been suffered by one of the bombers. Even so, they caused a great deal of fear and panic among the passengers.

On the Warren Street train, a young man was carrying a backpack when it exploded. It was a minor explosion, just large enough to blow open the backpack. One witness says that when the man with the

London police officers direct people away from a train station following a second series of attacks on the transit system.

backpack realized what had happened, "he made an exclamation as if something had gone wrong."[83]

One young man from Paris was reading a newspaper on the train and became distracted by the smell of burning rubber —probably from some part of the bomb. In moments, he says, everyone around him seemed to be alarmed by the smell, too.

"Suddenly people started screaming and were walking on each others' backs trying to get out of there," he says. "I couldn't move. I didn't know what to do. I saw what happened on July 7, and never thought it would happen to me. It was agonizing, those few seconds trying to get onto the platform [from the train]. Then we just ran."[84]

"It Was Like Champagne Popping"

The scene on the Oval station train was similar. Witnesses later said they saw a man with closed eyes and carrying a backpack

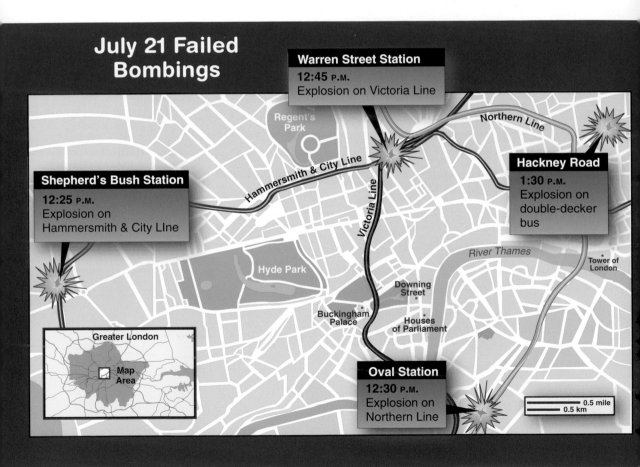

July 21 Failed Bombings

Warren Street Station
12:45 P.M.
Explosion on Victoria Line

Shepherd's Bush Station
12:25 P.M.
Explosion on Hammersmith & City LIne

Hackney Road
1:30 P.M.
Explosion on double-decker bus

Oval Station
12:30 P.M.
Explosion on Northern Line

Northern Line

Hammersmith & City Line

Victoria Line

Regent's Park

Hyde Park

River Thames

Downing Street

Buckingham Palace

Houses of Parliament

Tower of London

Greater London

Map Area

0.5 mile
0.5 km

who seemed to be praying. But there was no massive explosion, just a little smoke.

"I was in the carriage next to the one where the [backpack] was," one man recalls. "All of a sudden there was a popping. It sounded like champagne popping. I didn't think anything of it at the time, but then I heard a lot of people shouting from the carriage next door. People started saying, 'Get off the train, we're evacuating, everyone off.'"[85]

The bomber abandoned his smoking backpack and ran through an emergency door onto the platform. Three passengers chased the man, but they could not catch him.

"Are You All Right, Mate?"

Perhaps the most bizarre of the Underground bombings took place on the Shepherd's Bush train, west of downtown London. Again, witnesses report hearing the sound of a small explosion from passengers on the train. Abisha Moyo, a twenty-eight-year-old passenger from Zimbabwe, heard the noise and then noticed a man lying on the floor of the train car.

Moyo worried that the man had been injured. "I wasn't sure what had happened to him," he says, "and thought he might have been shot. I went up to him and said, 'Are you all right, mate?' But he ignored me and kept his eyes shut. . . . He looked dazed and confused, and very shaken."[86]

It was not until Moyo noticed wires sticking out of the man's shirt that he realized he must be a suicide bomber. By that time, however, the bomber was on his feet and running to the door of the train. Like the bombers from the other two trains, he escaped before anyone could apprehend him.

"I Didn't Know What I Would Find"

Shortly after the three train explosions, a fourth bomb detonated. This one was carried in a backpack worn by a middle-aged man on the top deck of a No. 26 bus. The explosion broke a window and created a lot of smoke, but did little other damage.

The driver was turning a corner when he heard the noise. "My initial thought was that it sounded like a bomb," he told reporters. "I have never been so frightened as when I went up the stairs [of the bus]. After what had happened earlier this month, I didn't know what I would find."[87]

Though passengers on the bus were unhurt, they were crying and shaken as they fled the bus. As the sound of police sirens wailed throughout the city, Underground train service halted again, investigators cordoned off four new crime scenes, and a massive search for the four escaped bombers began.

"We Know Why These Things Are Done"

Prime Minister Tony Blair was meeting with Australian prime minister John Howard when he learned the news of the explosions. Though he was relieved that no one was killed, Blair stated that it was important that the attacks not be minimized. "We know why these things are done," he said. "They are done to scare people and frighten them. To make them anxious and worried. We have to react calmly and get on with our business as normal."[88]

Police were optimistic about apprehending suspects in these latest bombings. Because the devices did not fully explode, a great deal of forensic evidence was available to investigators. One police spokesman asked anyone who might have noticed anything suspicious to come forward, urging Londoners to be particularly vigilant in case the unsuccessful bombers were to try again. "We are keen to speak to anyone who might have seen anything," he said. "The public are our eyes and ears."[89]

A Public Shooting

Some investigators began viewing CCTV video, which had proved so helpful earlier. Others worked with the forensic evidence, such as the traces of explosive found at the four sites. A gym membership card with an address on it was found in one of the scorched backpacks, and a third group of investigators concentrated on monitoring the building at that address, hoping it was the home of at least one of the suspects.

The address turned out to be an apartment complex in a working-class neighborhood in Lambert, south of downtown London. On Friday, July 22, the day after the attempted bombings, police watched as a man emerged from the building. Police later explained that he looked suspi-cious because he was wearing a padded fleece jacket, far too heavy for July weather, which they believed could easily be concealing a bomb. He also wore a black baseball cap that obscured his facial features.

They followed the man as he boarded a bus for the Stockwell Underground station. After the man got off the bus at the train station, he descended on the escalator and headed for the train. Police said they yelled for him to stop, but that instead of stopping, he ran for the train. According to the official police account, the man hopped over the turnstile and jumped onto the train, and undercover agents, believing he was about to detonate a bomb, fell on top of him.

Witnesses later said they could see the terror in the man's eyes as he was surrounded and held down by his pursuers, who shot him between seven and eleven times in the head. As the shots were fired, many passengers fled the train, believing the undercover police were terrorists using guns instead of bombs. Within thirty seconds, the train was virtually empty and a man was lying on the floor of the car in a dark pool of his own blood.

The Wrong Man

In a statement to the press soon after the incident, Ian Blair explained that the man on the train, who was identified as twenty-seven year-old Jean Charles de Menezes, was directly linked to their ongoing investigation of the bombings. Asked what had made police target the man, Blair said that both his clothing and his behavior on that day had made officers very suspicious.

CCTV cameras recorded these images of men thought to be responsible for the second series of attacks, carried out on July 21, 2005.

Subsequent findings showed that the shooting had been a mistake. Menezes lived in the apartment complex police were watching, but not in the same apartment as the bombing suspects. He was an electrician, and on the day of his death he had been catching a train to take him to a job where he was to install a new fire alarm system. He was unarmed when he was shot.

"He rang me ... saying that he would be a little late because the tube lines weren't working properly," Menezes's coworker

Gesio de Avila said. But hours went by and Avila did not hear from his friend. "When he didn't call me, I called and called and called. I left messages on the voice message system.... All day I was worried."[90] Avila and others who knew Menezes were appalled when they learned he had been gunned down by police, who thought he was a suicide bomber. They said the young man was not a violent person, and that he was so frightened by the July 7 bombings that he began saving his money for a motorbike so he could avoid danger on the Underground trains.

"I told him to take care [when he left Brazil] in England . . . but he laughed," said his mother. "'It's a clean place, Mum. The people are educated. There's no violence in England. No one goes around carrying guns. Not even the police.'"[91]

"This Is a Tragedy"

When police realized they had shot an innocent man, Ian Blair publicly apologized for the mistake. "This is a tragedy," he said. "The Metropolitan Police accepts full responsibility for this. To the family I can only express my deep regrets."[92] However, Blair warned that Menezes's death might not be the only casualty in the new war on terror in London.

Blair explained that the police were working under the rules of Operation Kratos, an aggressive antiterrorism format developed by the British shortly the attacks on the United States on September 11, 2001. Special opera-

"At the End of the Day, It Is Murder"

Soon after the tragic killing of a young Brazilian man mistaken for a suicide bomber on July 22, 2005, the Manchester Guardian *asked several experts their opinion of the police department's new "shoot-to-kill" policy. In an article titled "Is the Met's Shoot-To-Kill Policy Justified?" one Scottish human rights lawyer offers his thoughts.*

"Shoot to kill is justified only if you get the right person. It is never justified in any situation where someone is unarmed. Real questions have to be asked. I understand the situation where if someone is carrying a bomb and looks as if they are about to detonate it, but this man was followed and chased. On what basis did they shoot to kill? There has to be public accountability.

"To think what was going through that man's thoughts in his last moments, being executed—five shots—it was an execution, and at the end of the day, it is murder. What else could it be called? They shot an innocent man. It is not good enough to say, 'we apologize, it's a tragedy.' Tomorrow it could be someone else's father, brother, sister that could be shot in similar circumstances."

A mourner kneels at a makeshift shrine dedicated to a young Brazilian immigrant whom police mistakenly shot to death.

tions groups within the Metropolitan Police force developed a "shoot to kill" strategy when dealing with suspected terrorists.

London police, who historically had never carried firearms, were now authorized to shoot any suspect they believed to be a suicide bomber. Blair explained that in such cases, police were instructed to shoot at the suspect's head. "There is no point in shooting in someone's chest, because that is where the bomb is likely to be," he said. "There is no point in shooting anywhere else if they fall down and detonate it. The only way to deal with this is to shoot to the head."[93]

Prime Minister Tony Blair was supportive of the police, although he acknowledged a tragic mistake had occurred. The police were risking their lives, operating under a great deal of danger and uncertainty, he said. "Had the circumstances been different and this had turned out to be a terrorist, and [the police] had failed to take action, they would have been criticized the other way."[94]

Protesters in London march in response to the killing of Jean Charles de Menezes, whom police mistook for a would-be suicide bomber.

"What's Happening to My City?"

Not all Londoners were as understanding. A representative of the Muslim Council of Britain felt that the police needed to be clearer about their policy. "There may be a reason why the police felt it necessary to unload five shots [later found to be between seven and eleven] into the man and shoot him dead," he said, "but they need to make those reasons clear. Quite a lot of Muslims are distressed about . . . the 'shoot to kill' policy."[95]

Other Londoners expressed uneasiness about London's changed atmosphere. "You've got sirens that never stop, police with rifles and machine guns everywhere," said Catherine Wilson, a retired headmistress. "It never seems to stop. It just feels dangerous now, and never did particularly before."[96]

Patrice Clark, a bank supervisor, agreed that the city had experienced a radical change within a two-week period, and that the change frightened her. "I think every large city has a particular feel to it," she said. "Just the rhythm of it, the noises, the traffic, and so on. London was always an exciting place to live, very alive. But it feels very different to me now, more sinister somehow. I worry that something irrevocable has happened to our city, and that we may never get it back as it was. That's a terrible thought."[97]

Others agreed, saying that the government's concern that there were more al Qaeda cells in London just waiting to strike again was terrifying. In a very short period, London had gone from being a city in the midst of celebration to a city under siege, and no one was quite certain how long this unsettling new feeling would last.

Chapter Five

What's Next?

The response from the British government and law enforcement to the bombings was to implement strong new antiterrorism measures, many of which were aimed at making public transportation less vulnerable to attacks. One very visible change was an increase in police presence at all Underground stations. Some police worked with bomb-sniffing dogs that are trained to react to the slightest trace of an explosive. Many of the police officers in the Underground were part of the Metropolitan Police, but British Transport Police and undercover officers took part as well.

The show of strength was especially strong on Thursdays in the months following the bombings, since both attacks had occurred on that day. More than six thousand officers patrolled the Underground, talking with passengers and adding what was intended to be a reassuring presence. Several officers said that it was gratifying for them because travelers seemed to genuinely appreciate that they were on duty, and they received many smiles and greetings.

Some of the new police procedures were not as universally appreciated, however. Officers had been instructed to stop and search anyone who appeared suspicious, and, not surprisingly, some passengers felt they were being singled out because they were not white. One young British television researcher was saddened because he was treated as a suspect. Ironically, he says, he had been very proud of the way his city bounced back from the July 7 bombings.

"I never felt more proud of being British and being a Londoner," he says. "I went away for two weeks on holiday and when I came back, I never felt more like an alien. On the buses and on the trains the seat next to me is often empty. I feel like a pariah. If this continues, it is hard to imagine how I could live a normal life."[98]

Increasing the Number of Cameras

Another weapon against terrorism is the constant surveillance by London's CCTV cameras. Plans were already in place to add between three thousand and six thousand new cameras in the Underground before the 2012 Olympic Games. Because of the new terrorist threat, however, the government decided to begin installing them sooner.

The cameras themselves are of a higher grade than ever before. American reporter Sharon Schmickle notes that the cameras installed in the CCTV system are far superior to those commonly used in the United States, writing, "Forget the fuzzy images you have seen in some crime shots from [American] convenience stores; these state-of-the-art cameras produce broadcast-quality images."[99]

In addition to increasing the number of cameras in the Underground, the government has added more attendants in the station that monitors them. An attendant in the CCTV control room can follow the movements of a particular traveler walking

A London police officer, assisted by a bomb-sniffing dog, keeps watch as commuters walk along a train station platform.

A police officer keeps an eye on a bank of monitors connected to some of the cameras located in many of the public spaces in London.

through the station, riding an escalator, or purchasing a ticket before boarding the train.

Schmickle watched as attendants zoomed in on three men carrying suitcases as they headed to a train's boarding platform. The attendants watched carefully to make sure none of the men left a suitcase behind— a possible bombing scenario. "If any of them left a bag behind," she explains, "the station would have to be closed and evacuated immediately. The men picked up the bags, though, and boarded the next train."[100]

Some people don't care for the elaborate surveillance system. They say that it feels like something out of George Orwell's *1984*, a book in which Big Brother government is always monitoring the movements of it citizens. One British civil rights group opposed to the cameras has called for people to attack the cameras with glue, spray paint, and even laser guns. But the majority of Londoners are used to the cameras and rarely give them a second thought. "We don't get too paranoid about the cameras," says one. "In fact, most people just ignore them."[101]

Laws to Help Stop Terrorism

Part of the new plan to stop terrorism in Britain was the enactment of several laws that make it easier for law enforcement to investigate and arrest terrorists. For example, in the days after the bombings, Tony Blair called on Britain's judges to allow police to detain suspected terrorists, holding them indefinitely without a trial. (The current rule is that no suspect may be detained for more than fourteen days without being charged with a crime.)

Blair told the judges that the September 11 attacks on the United States should have motivated America's allies to install new antiterrorist measures, but Britain had not heeded the call. He warned them that the world had dropped its guard since those attacks, and terrorists were capitalizing on their negligence. "September 11 for me was a wake-up call," he said. "Do you know what I think the problem is? That a lot of the world woke up for a short time and then turned over and went back to sleep again."[102]

Bomb Web Sites and Tapped Phones

Law enforcement officials spoke out in favor of a proposed law that would allow police officers to tap terror suspects' telephone calls, monitor their e-mails, and even intercept their mail if officers felt it would help them prevent an attack. One supporter of that legislation said it would not even be necessary for police to tap every call or screen every e-mail: Just the fear that the communication might be monitored could be enough to drive the terrorists into the open. "If criminals believe that every call they make is tapped because it could be," he explained, "they will meet more, leave their houses, [and] go under CCTV cameras."[103]

Some experts have expressed concern about terrorists' ability to get information over the Internet. Scores of Web sites provide step-by-step instructions for making a wide variety of explosives. After the bombings, Britain's Association of Chief Police

The Ways We Cope

In his London Times *commentary "Fear? We're Revelling in It," Frank Furedi talks about some of the strategies he and others found helpful as a way of dealing with fear after the London bombings.*

"As we become accustomed to living with fear, we develop coping strategies:

We use our mobile phones in a different way. We make more calls and text more frequently to let people know where we are, rather than just ringing for a chat.

We evaluate information differently. When we first got emails warning us of viruses, most people notified everyone in their address book. Now, as there are so many false alarms, we ignore them. This is similar to information we receive on terrorism. As time goes by and there are more false security alerts we will become more blase.

We no longer travel from A to B via the shortest route. Instead, we evaluate the different options and choose the one we think safest according to the information that we have. For example, we may avoid the Tube if we can get a lift instead."

Officers (ACPO) asked for legislation that would allow the removal of any Internet sites that might help potential terrorists.

Some Britons worried that the antiterrorist measures were going too far. The idea that the government could detain a suspect indefinitely or monitor someone's e-mails or telephone calls was unsettling. Many wondered whether in the process of fighting terror, Britain was compromising its citizens' right to privacy, to a fair trial, and other rights Britons hold dear. Some were concerned that such powers could be abused against citizens, and Britain could become a police state.

London newspaper commentator Mary Riddell addressed that very idea. She wrote that Tony Blair was insistent that people needed to get back to normal, to get on with their lives after the bombings. He urged that people must not change the way they lived, because to do so would be letting the terrorists win. But it is possible that abandoning British laws gives the terrorists an even bigger victory. "Being normal means being free," she wrote. "And that, in turn, involves ensuring that the laws and principles which enshrine liberty are not overturned in the months to come."[104]

A Terror Tax

As Britons continued to debate the best tactics for thwarting terrorism, they also had to examine how to pay for these efforts. Two bombing investigations in two weeks strained the law enforcement budget. The cost of the investigations in late July ran at more that £500,000 per day, as more than one thousand police officers worked twelve-hour shifts, seven days a week. Even though the bombers of July 7 had been killed by their own bombs, counterterrorism investigators tried to find out what connections, if any, they had to other terrorists. Police work on the July 21 bombings continued, too, and an ever-increasing list of suspected accomplices was thoroughly investigated.

The immediate needs of police in the two terrorism cases required the efforts of hundreds of officers taken from departments such as homicide, organized crime, and drugs. This left a mere fraction of the needed police available to work on other crimes. It was clear that more police, and more funds to pay them, were needed.

"We are in consultation with central government for extra funding," one police source explained. "Obviously we have not got infinite resources and we will have to find the money from somewhere."[105] The source of the revenue, police and lawmakers hoped, would come from a new tax, known as the Terror Tax, that would pay for increased security measures and salaries for additional police officers.

Some Londoners complained about the proposed tax, saying they were already taxed far too much. But others noted that there was very little choice, since fighting terrorism was crucial for Britain's survival. "It's important to have security," one Londoner said, "and if we have to contribute to the cost of it, it's not a bad thing. The money has to come from somewhere."[106]

"Set Your Own House in Order"

While politicians and police considered new antiterrorist tools and legislation, some Londoners wondered whether there might be another way of getting at the problem of terrorism by extremist Muslims. Perhaps, they suggested, it would also be helpful to get to the source of the problem.

Britain has long been criticized by the international community for allowing radicals and supporters of terrorism from North Africa and the Middle East into the country at the same time Britain's allies were working to keep such people out.

The Saudi Arabian ambassador to Britain, for example, has frequently commented that it is far too easy for Islamic extremists to stay in London and preach messages of hate without having to worry about being deported or put in jail. The president of Pakistan, the nation from which many of London's Muslim dissidents have emigrated, warned, "Please set your own house in order. I would like to say there is a lot to be done by Pakistan [in controlling terrorism] and, may I suggest, that there is a lot to be done in England also."[107]

Britain has preferred to tolerate the presence of extremists, as long as they obeyed the laws. However, many world

Police interview a resident of the British city of Birmingham as part of their ongoing investigation of the July 21, 2005, terrorist attacks.

leaders complain that British officials have done little to monitor the activities of extremists, arguing that while they may not be breaking British laws outwardly, they are using London as a recruiting and operations center for terror elsewhere.

"They Decided to . . . Send the First Blast"

After the September 11, 2001, attacks on the United States, Britain's policy changed somewhat. Law enforcement officers began to monitor suspected extremist cells and even detained some radical imams (Muslim clerics) who were suspected of supporting a jihad, or holy war, against the West.

Because of such new policies, and especially because of Britain's participation in the U.S.-led war against Iraq, which began in 2003, intelligence experts say there has been a change in the way Islamic radicals talk about Britain, especially on the extremist Web sites. "[T]he tone and the language . . . has changed completely with regards to Great Britain," says one Middle East expert. "Once [terrorists] felt that the British are going after them significantly,

"I Don't Sit at the Top of the Bus"

After the London bombings, the Children's Express Web site encouraged young people and their parents to share their thoughts about how their lives had changed. The following is a sample of the responses released in the August 3, 2005, edition of Children's Express, called "Life After the London Bombings."

"Seri Davies, 18, lives in North London and says she will probably never get on the Tube again. 'I still use the bus, but I'm a lot more wary. For short journeys I tend to walk now. After the [July 7] bombing I was a bit wary expecially as the first bus I got on was the number 30, but now I'm more at ease. . . . I definitely am more vigilant. I look around more when I'm alone, I don't sit at the top of the bus, and I don't sit at the back.

My parents are a lot more cautious and always ask me where I am. Straight after the attacks, my mum was like, don't go around King's Cross for awhile. My parents haven't told me not to use public transport because it's the only way that I can get from A to B. But, they do say be careful and be aware, and if I see anything suspicious, get off.'

But some parents have even stopped their children using public transportation altogether. . . . Ten-year-old . . . Giovana . . . says because of her mum's ban she's missing out on stuff: "I feel a bit annoyed because we could have gone to the science museum or the natural history museum by the bus or the train. . . . I don't think she is overreacting, though, she is just doing it to keep us safe.'"

they decided to go ahead and send the first blast."[108]

Although authorities are unclear exactly what organization, if any, was behind the suicide bombings of July 7 and the failed attacks of July 22, it is obvious that a large group of young British Muslims has emerged, motivated by radical Muslim thinking and ready to wage its own jihad. And because many of them are clean skins, there is little chance of identifying them beforehand. "You can jail all the imams you want—in London or wherever," says one international relations expert, "but how can you round up all the young men and possibly some young women they've roused to their cause? The answer is simple—you can't."[109]

"They're the Real Serious Muslims, Man"

Most of London's Muslim population is moderate, but they acknowledge that more and more young Muslims are turning to the ideas of the radical imams. Interestingly, many of these young people are second- or third-generation Londoners who are rejecting some of the ideas of their parents, saying they feel out of place in Western culture—and equally out of place visiting extended family back in the Middle East. "When you visit Pakistan," one says, "you're seen as a spoiled brat from the west. Here, they call you a Paki."[110]

Many British Muslims feel left out and isolated from other young people. They cannot totally embrace many aspects of Western teenage culture because of the strictness of their religion. They also feel alienated because of the British government's enthusiastic support of the war in Iraq. They hear their prime minister urging young Brits to join the army and fight in Iraq, and it hurts because it is Muslims who are the enemy in that war.

Some Muslim youth find the actions of the terrorists exciting, even heroic. One young man believes terrorists are the ultimate heroes, risking their lives to fight against injustice faced by Muslims throughout the world. "They're the real serious Muslims, man," says the twenty-five-year-old London factory worker. "I'll do *jihad* if *jihad* comes to Britain."[111]

"You Don't Want a Vacuum"

Some Muslim moderates believe terrorism in London can be eliminated only by reaching out to these disenfranchised young people. "We need to find the common ground," says one London Muslim. "Unity is what brings people together. You don't want a vacuum because then real extremists will fill it."[112]

Some Muslims have been critical of the Muslim leaders Tony Blair has asked to publicly condemn terror. These leaders, referred to as "Tony's Cronies" by many Muslims who feel they are brought in front of cameras simply to repeat the prime minister's views, do not resonate with young people. It would be better, say some, to engage leaders who appeal to younger Muslims to speak for peace. One newspaper columnist suggested Muslim boxing star Amir Khan and singer-songwriter Yusuf

Members of the Muslim Association of Britain march at a rally to voice their opposition to extremist violence.

Islam, two individuals who would undoubtedly energize many young Muslims in a positive way.

Robert Springborg, the director of the London Middle East Institute, agrees that it is critically important to reach out to disenfranchised Muslims. "There is nothing you can do to force that," he says. "You can't have a government policy of making friends, so forget that one. But you can have a government policy that does try to draw people into the political system and the economy. If you do that, then I think they might be drawn into the social system."[113]

Muslims and non-Muslims alike say that the fight to reclaim their city from the threat of terrorism will be a difficult one, and could take years—or even decades. While there may be debate over which weapons to use in that struggle, there is no question about the need to avoid a repeat of the London bombings of July 2005.

Notes

Introduction: The Bloodiest Day

1. Tara O'Beirn, personal interview, November 2, 2005.

Chapter One: What a Difference a Day Makes

2. Quoted in Tom Knott, "Britain's Perfect Moment Shattered All Too Quickly," *Washington Times*, July 8, 2005, p. C1.

3. Quoted in Robert Barr, "London Basks in Olympic Glow," *Fort Wayne* (IN) *Journal -Gazette*, July 7, 2005, p. A1.

4. Robin, telephone interview, October 18, 2005.

5. Quoted in Olga Craig, "We Saw the Best of Things and the Worst," *Sunday Telegraph* (London), July 10, 2005, p. 14.

6. Quoted in Craig, "We Saw the Best of Things," p. 14.

7. Quoted in Evan Thomas and Stryker McGuire, "Terror at Rush Hour," *Newsweek*, July 18, 2005, p. 31.

8. Quoted in Craig, "We Saw the Best of Things," p. 14.

9. Quoted in *Cambridge Evening News*, "I Was in the Tube Bomb Carriage—and Survived," July 11, 2005. www.cambridge news.co.uk/news/region_wide/2005/07 /11/83e33146-09-af-4421-b2f41779a86 926f9.1pf.

10. Quoted in Robert Mason Lee, "'I Have Just Seen Hell,'" *Maclean's*, July 18, 2005, p. 14.

11. Quoted in Michael Elliott, "Rush Hour Terror," *Time*, July 18, 2005, p. 35.

12. Quoted in Miles Kemp, "This Is Death, Thought SA Survivor of London Blast," *Advertiser* (Adelaide), September 29, 2005, p. 28.

13. Quoted in Lee, "'I Have Just Seen Hell,'" p. 14.

14. Quoted in Lee, "'I Have Just Seen Hell,'" p. 14.

15. Quoted in Lee, "'I Have Just Seen Hell,'" p. 14.

16. Quoted in Kemp, "This Is Death," p. 28.

17. Quoted in *BBC News*, "Coming Together as a City," July 15, 2005. http://news.bbc. co.uk/1/hi/uk/4670099.stm.

18. Name withheld, personal interview with the author, August 4, 2005, St. Paul, MN.

19. Terry Kirby, personal interview, July 23, 2005, London.

20. Quoted in Thomas and McGuire, "Terror at Rush Hour," p. 33.

21. Quoted in Craig, "We Saw the Best of Things," p. 14.

22. Quoted in Elliott, "Rush Hour Terror," p. 30.

23. Quoted in Craig, "We Saw the Best of Things," p. 14.

24. Andrew Dearden, "The Bus, the Purse, and the Limb," *British Medical Journal*, July 16, 2005.

25. Quoted in Craig, "We Saw the Best of Things," p. 14.

26. Quoted in Craig, "We Saw the Best of Things," p. 14.

Chapter Two: "We Shall Prevail"

27. Quoted in Lee, "'I Have Just Seen Hell,'" p. 14.

28. Quoted in CNN, "Terror in London," July 7, 2005.

29. Quoted in Neil McIntosh, "Bomb Blasts Plunge London into Chaos," *Guardian Unlimited*, July 7, 2005. http://blogs.guardian.co.uk/news/archives/2005/07/07/bomb_blasts_plunge_london_into_chaos.html.

30. Quoted in J.F.O. McAllister, "How Tony Blair Found His Groove," *Time*, July 18, 2005, p. 35.

31. Quoted in Matthew Schofield, "Life Continues Return to Normal in London," *Knight Ridder/Tribune News Service*, July 10, 2005, p. 1.

32. Quoted in Judy Keen, "To Get On with Our Lives Is a Matter of Pride," *USA Today*, July 11, 2005, p. A8.

33. Quoted in Keen, "To Get On with Our Lives," p. A8.

34. Quoted in Keen, "To Get On with Our Lives," p. A8.

35. Quoted in Lizette Alvarez, "Photos Plead, 'Have You Seen This Person?'" *New York Times*, July 10, 2005, p. A1.

36. Quoted in Alvarez, "Photos Plead," p. A1.

37. Quoted in *St. Petersburg Times*, "Pathologists Begin Identifying London Blast Victims," July 12, 2005, p. 1A.

38. Quoted in Carol Williams, "Tea and Sympathy, but Little News on the Missing," *Los Angeles Times*, July 10, 2005, p. A10.

39. Quoted in Williams, "Tea and Sympathy," p. A10.

40. Quoted in Amanda Friedman, "Terrorist Attacks on London Affect More than Just Pubs, Restaurants," *Nation's Restaurant News*, August 1, 2005, p. 50.

41. Harold, personal interview, July 25, London.

42. Quoted in *Age* (Melbourne), "Blast Survivor Still Looking for Answers," September 21, 2005. www.theage.com.au/news/World/Blastsurvivorstilllookingforanswers/2005/09/21/1126982083721.html.

43. Daphna Baram, "Suddenly, Living in London Reminds Me of Being in Jerusalem," *Guardian* (Manchester), July 22, 2005, p. 5.

44. Quoted in Tamara Jones, "King's Cross Station, London's Underground Zero," *Washington Post*, July 24, 2005, D1.

45. Quoted in *BBC News*, "Coming Together as a City."

46. Quoted in Karen Hunter, "After Attack, Blog Brought London to Life," *Hartford Courant*, July 17, 2005, p. C3.

47. Quoted in *BBC News*, "Coming Together as a City."

Chapter Three: Investigating Four Bombings

48. Quoted in Jason Bennetto, "Hunt for the Bombers," *Independent* (London), July 12, 2005, p. 9.

49. Quoted in David Kaplan and Thomas Grose, "On the Terrorists' Trail," *U.S. News & World Report*, July 25, 2005, p. 22.

50. Name withheld, personal interview with the author, August 4, 2005, St. Paul, MN.

51. Quoted in CNN, "London Terror," July 10, 2005.

52. Craig Smith, "Inches at a Time, Crews

Search for Bodies in a London Tunnel," *New York Times*, July 11, 2005, p. A1.

53. Quoted in Lee, "'I Have Just Seen Hell,'" p. 14.

54. Quoted in Glenn Frankel, "Londoners Warily Resume Their Lives," *Washington Post*, July 9, 2005, p. A1.

55. Quoted in Smith, "Inches at a Time," p. A1.

56. Quoted in *CNN.com*, "Group Lays Claim to London Blasts," July 8, 2005. www.cnn.com/2005/WORLD/europe/07/07/explosions.claim/index.html.

57. Quoted in *CNN.com*, "Group Lays Claim to London Blasts."

58. Quoted in Kevin Whitelaw, Thomas Grose, and Gilian Sandford, "Terror on the Thames," *U.S. News & World Report*, July 18, 2005, p. 20.

59. Quoted in Ian Cobain, "Suicide Bomb Theory After Anxious Passenger Report," *Guardian* (Manchester), July 9, 2005, p. 5.

60. Quoted in CNN, "London Terror," July 15, 2005.

61. Quoted in Bennetto, "Hunt for the Bombers," p. 9.

62. Quoted in CNN, "London Terror," July 9, 2005.

63. Quoted in Kaplan and Grose, "On the Terrorists' Trail," p. 22.

64. Quoted in Tara Pepper and Mark Hosenball, "A Deadly Puzzle," *Newsweek*, July 25, 2005, p. 41.

65. Quoted in Scheherezade Faramarzi, "Brits Suspected in Attacks Led 'Normal' Lives," *Houston Chronicle*, July 14, 2005, p. 1.

66. Quoted in Faramarzi, "Brits Suspected in Attacks," p. 1.

67. Quoted in Kaplan and Grose, "On the Terrorists' Trail," p. 23.

Chapter Four: More Violence in the City

68. Joseph, personal interview, July 26, 2005, London.

69. Quoted in *RingSurf.com*, "London Bombing," July 8, 2005. www.ringsurf.com/forum/answers-London_bombing_terrorist.

70. Quoted in *RingSurf.com*, "London Bombing."

71. Quoted in Terri Judd, Nigel Morris, Ian Herbert, and Paul Kelbie, "Britain's Muslim Scapegoats," *Belfast Telegraph*, August 4, 2005, p. 1.

72. Quoted in Judd et al., "Britain's Muslim Scapegoats," p. 1.

73. Quoted in Ellen Knickmeyer, "Muslim Woman Becomes Symbol Among the Missing," *Wall Street Journal*, July 13, 2005, p. A3.

74. Quoted in Knickmeyer, "Muslim Woman Becomes Symbol," p. A3.

75. Quoted in Arifa Akbar and Genevieve Roberts, "Reaction in Yorkshire," *Independent* (London), July 13, 2005, p. 5.

76. Quoted in Judd, et al., "Britain's Muslim Scapegoats," p. 1.

77. Quoted in Calum McDonald, "Young, Muslim, and Facing a New World of Shaken Beliefs," *Herald* (Glasgow), July 16, 2005, p. 10.

78. Quoted in McDonald, "Young, Muslim, and Facing a New World," p. 10.

79. Quoted in Alan Cowell, "Show of Resolve as Religious Leaders Try to Cool Ten-

sions," *New York Times*, July 11, 2005, p. A9.

80. Quoted in Cowell, "Show of Resolve," p. A9.

81. Quoted in Judd et al., "Britain's Muslim Scapegoats," p. 1.

82. Quoted in Judd et al., "Britain's Muslim Scapegoats," p. 1.

83. Quoted in Christine Spolar and Tom Hundley, "Clues Sought in Latest Wave of Bombings," *South Florida Sun-Sentinel*, July 22, 2005, p. 10A.

84. Quoted in Andrew Alderson, "Business as Usual?" *Sunday Telegraph* (London), July 24, 2005, p. 16.

85. Quoted in Spolar and Hundley, "Clues Sought," p. 10A.

86. Quoted in Alderson, "Business as Usual?" p. 16.

87. Quoted in Alderson, "Business as Usual?" p. 16.

88. Quoted in Spolar and Hundley, "Clues Sought," p. 10A.

89. Quoted in Spolar and Hundley, "Clues Sought," p. 10A.

90. Quoted in *Guardian* (Manchester), "Short Walk and the No. 2 Bus," July 25, 2005, p. 1.

91. Quoted in *Guardian*, "Short Walk and the No. 2 Bus," p. 1.

92. Quoted in Rosie Cowan, Vikram Dodd, and Richard Norton-Taylor, "Met Chief Warns More Could be Shot," *Guardian*, July 25, 2005, p. 1.

93. Quoted in Cowan, "Met Chief Warns More Could be Shot," p. 1.

94. Quoted in Sarah Lyall, "Terror War Takes Another Innocent Life," *Houston Chronicle*, July 26, 2005, p. 8.

95. Quoted in *Sunday Times* (London), "Hair Trigger Tragedy," July 24, 2005, p. 18.

96. Catherine Wilson, personal interview, July 25, 2005, London.

97. Patrice Clark, personal interview, July 28, 2005, London.

Chapter Five: What's Next?

98. Quoted in Robert Mendick, "Asians Divided by Police Stop and Search Powers," *Evening Standard* (London), August 3, 2005, p. 9.

99. Sharon Schmickle, "Eye on Security," *Minneapolis Star Tribune*, October 17, 2005, p. A11.

100. Quoted in Schmickle, "Eye on Security," p. A11.

101. Quoted in Schmickle, "Eye on Security," p. A11.

102. Quoted in Phillip Webster, "World 'Turned Over and Went Back to Sleep After 9/11 Wake-Up Call,'" *Times* (London), July 27, 2005, p. 4.

103. Quoted in S.A. Mathieson, "Site Surveillance," *Guardian* (Manchester), August 4, 2005, p. 14.

104. Mary Riddell, "Hope and Fear in the City," *Observer* (London), July 24, 2005, p. 26.

105. Quoted in Stewart Tendler, Michael Evans, and Richard Ford, "Londoners Face Terror Tax to Pay for Extra Police," *Times* (London), August 3, 2005. www.timesonline.co.uk/article/0,,22080-1718983_2,00html.

106. Quoted in Mark Harrington, "London Adjusts to Life After Bombings," *Newsday*, August 5, 2005, p. A28.

107. Quoted in Tom Baldwin, "Global Call to End the Era of 'Londonistan,'" *Times*, (London), July 23, 2005, p. 11.

108. Quoted in Elliott, "Rush Hour Terror," p. 37.

109. Fantu, personal interview, October 13, 2005, Minneapolis.

110. Quoted in Carla Power, "The Lost Generation," *Newsweek*, August, 15, 2005, p. 21.

111. Quoted in Power, "The Lost Generation," p. 21.

112. Quoted in Jimmy Burns, Stephen Fidler, and Roula Khalaf, "From Disaffection to Deathly Destruction," *Financial Times*, July 14, 2005, p. 17.

113. Quoted in Sharon Schmickle, "Wrestling with the Enemy Within," *Minneapolis Star Tribune*, October 24, 2005, p. A1.

For Further Reading

Books

Thomas M. Collins, *Tony Blair.*
Minneapolis: Lerner, 2005. A very
interesting biography of Britain's prime
minister, with a complete index.

Phillip Margulies, *Al Qaeda: Osama bin
Laden's Army of Terrorists.* New York:
Rosen, 2003. A readable account of the
world's most dangerous terrorist
organization, with a helpful
bibliography.

Gail Stewart, *Crime Scene Investigation:
Bombings.* San Diego, CA: Lucent, 2006.
A look at how investigators and forensic
teams go about solving bombings.

Periodicals

Michael Elliott, "Rush Hour Terror," *Time*,
July 18, 2005.

David Kaplan and Thomas Grose, "On the
Terrorists' Trail," *U.S. News & World
Report*, July 25, 2005.

Evan Thomas and Stryker McGuire, "Terror
at Rush Hour," *Newsweek*, July 18, 2005.

Web Sites

BBC News, "In Depth: London Attacks."
(http://news.bbc.co.uk/1/hi/in
depth/uk/2005/london_explosions/de
fault.stm). A very complete website,
with video reactions by witnesses,
photographs of the individuals killed in
the four attacks, and up-to-date
information on the status of the
investigation of the July 21 bombings.

London Underground (www.tfl.gov.uk/
tube/). This site contains maps, detailed
information on each train line, and
background on the underground
subway system.

PBS: Frontline, *Hunting bin Laden*
(www.pbs.org/wgbh/pages/frontline/
shows/binladen). This site contains
background on Osama bin Laden and
his al Qaeda terror organization as well
as a chronology of al Qaeda terrorist
activities and investigations into those
crimes.

Works Consulted

Periodicals

Arifa Akbar and Genevieve Roberts, "Reaction in Yorkshire," *Independent* (London), July 13, 2005.

Andrew Alderson, "Business as Usual?" *Sunday Telegraph* (London), July 24, 2005.

Lizette Alvarez, "Photos Plead, 'Have You Seen This Person?'" *New York Times*, July 10, 2005.

Tom Baldwin, "Global Call to End the Era of 'Londonistan,'" *Times* (London), July 23, 2005.

Daphna Baram, "Suddenly, Living in London Reminds Me of Being in Jerusalem," *Guardian* (Manchester), July 22, 2005.

Robert Barr, "London Basks in Olympic Glow," *Fort Wayne* (IN) *Journal-Gazette*, July 7, 2005.

Jason Bennetto, "Hunt for the Bombers," *Independent* (London), July 12, 2005.

Jimmy Burns, Stephen Fidler, and Roula Khalaf, "From Disaffection to Deathly Destruction," *Financial Times*, July 14, 2005.

CNN, "London Terror," July 7–15, 2005.

Ian Cobain, "Suicide Bomb Theory after Anxious Passenger Report," *Guardian* (Manchester), July 9, 2005.

Rosie Cowan, Vikram Dodd, and Richard Norton-Taylor, "Met Chief Warns More Could be Shot," *Guardian* (Manchester), July, 25, 2005.

Alan Cowell, "Show of Resolve as Religious Leaders Try to Cool Tensions," *New York Times*, July 11, 2005.

Olga Craig, "We Saw the Best of Things and the Worst," *Sunday Telegraph* (London), July 10, 2005.

Andrew Dearden, "The Bus, the Purse, and the Limb," *British Medical Journal*, July 16, 2005.

Scheherezade Faramarzi, "Brits Suspected in Attacks Led 'Normal' Lives," *Houston Chronicle*, July 14, 2005.

David Frabotta, "Surviving London," *DVM*, September 2005.

Glenn Frankel, "Londoners Warily Resume Their Lives," *Washington Post*, July 9, 2005.

Amanda Friedman, "Terrorist Attacks on London Affect More than Just Pubs, Restaurants," *Nation's Restaurant News*, August 1, 2005.

Frank Furedi, "Fear? We're Revelling in It," *Time* (London), July 30, 2005.

Charlotte Gill, "Will Their Smiles Ever Be Seen Again?" *Daily Mail*, July 11, 2005.

Guardian (Manchester), "Is the Met's Shoot-to-Kill Policy Justified?" July 25, 2005.

———, "Short Walk and the No. 2 Bus," July 25, 2005.

Mark Harrington, "London Adjusts to Life After Bombings," *Newsday*, August 5, 2005.

Karen Hunter, "After Attack, Blog Brought London to Life," *Hartford Courant*, July 17, 2005.

Tamara Jones, "King's Cross Station, London's Underground Zero," *Washington Post*, July 24, 2005.

Terri Judd, Nigel Morris, Ian Herbert, and Paul Kelbie, "Britain's Muslim Scapegoats," *Belfast Telegraph*, August 4, 2005.

Judy Keen, "To Get on with Our Lives Is a Matter of Pride," *USA Today*, July 11, 2005.

Miles Kemp, "This Is Death, Thought SA Survivor of London Blast," *Advertiser* (Adelaide), September 29, 2005.

Ellen Knickmeyer, "Muslim Woman Becomes Symbol Among the Missing," *Wall Street Journal*, July 13, 2005.

Tom Knott, "Britain's Perfect Moment Shattered All Too Quickly," *Washington Times*, July 8, 2005.

Robert Mason Lee, "'I Have Just Seen Hell,'" *Maclean's*, July 18, 2005.

Sarah Lyall, "Terror War Takes Another Innocent Life," *Houston Chronicle*, July 26, 2005.

S.A. Mathieson, "Site Surveillance," *Guardian* (Manchester), August 4, 2005.

J.F.O. McAllister, "How Tony Blair Found His Groove," *Time*, July 18, 2005.

Calum McDonald, "Young, Muslim, and Facing a New World of Shaken Beliefs," *Herald* (Glasgow), July 16, 2005.

Robert Mendick, "Asians Divided by Police Stop and Search Powers," *Evening Standard* (London), August 3, 2005.

Tara Pepper and Mark Hosenball, "A Deadly Puzzle," *Newsweek*, July 25, 2005.

Carla Power, "The Lost Generation," *Newsweek*, August, 15, 2005.

Mary Riddell, "Hope and Fear in the City," *Observer* (London), July 24, 2005.

St. Petersburg Times, "Pathologists Begin Identifying London Blast Victims," July 12, 2005.

Sharon Schmickle, "Eye on Security," *Minneapolis Star Tribune*, October 17, 2005.

———, "Wrestling with the Enemy Within," *Minneapolis Star Tribune*, October 24, 2005.

Matthew Schofield, "Life Continues Return to Normal in London," *Knight Ridder/ Tribune News Service*, July 10, 2005.

Craig Smith, "Inches at a Time, Crews Search for Bodies in a London Tunnel," *New York Times*, July 11, 2005.

Christine Spolar and Tom Hundley, "Clues Sought in Latest Wave of Bombings," *South Florida Sun-Sentinel*, July 22, 2005.

Sunday Times (London), "Hair Trigger Tragedy," July 24, 2005.

Phillip Webster, "World 'Turned Over and Went Back to Sleep After 9/11 Wake-Up Call,'" *Times* (London), July 27, 2005.

Kevin Whitelaw, Thomas Grose, and Gilian Sandford, "Terror on the Thames," *U.S. News & World Report*, July 18, 2005.

Carol Williams, "Tea and Sympathy, but Little News on the Missing," *Los Angeles Times*, July 10, 2005.

Internet Sources

Age (Melbourne), "Blast Survivor Still

Looking for Answers," September 21, 2005. www.theage.com.au/news/World/ Blastsurvivorstilllookingfor answers/ 2005/09/21/1126982083721.html.

BBC News, "Coming Together as a City," July 15, 2005. http://news.bbc.co.uk/ 1/hi/uk/ 4670099.stm.

Cambridge Evening News, "I Was in the Tube Bomb Carriage—and Survived," July 11, 2005. www.cambridge-news. co.uk/news/region wide/2005/07/11/ 83e33146-09-af-4421-b2f4-1779a86926 f9.1pf.

Children's Express, "Life After the London Bombings," August 3, 2005. www. childrens-express.org/dynamic/ public/Life after london_bombings 180805.html.

CNN.com, "Group Lays Claim to London Blasts," July 8, 2005.www.cnn.com/2005/ WORLD/europe/07/07/explosions.claim / index.html.

Neil McIntosh, "Bomb Blasts Plunge London into Chaos," *Guardian Unlimited*, July 7, 2005. http://blogs. guardian.co.uk/news/archives/2005/07/ 07/bomb_blasts_plunge_london_into_c haos.html.

———, "Your Messages of Support," *Guardian Unlimited*, July 8, 2005.http:// blogs.guardian.co.uk/news/archives/200 5/07/08/your_messages_Of_support.html

RingSurf.com, "London Bombing," July 8, 2005. www.ringsurf.com/forum/ answers-London_bombing_terrorist.

Stewart Tendler, Michael Evans, and Richard Ford, "Londoners Face Terror Tax to Pay for Extra Police," *Times* (London), August 3, 2005. www.timesonline.co.uk/ article/0,,22080-1718983 2,00html.

Index

Picture Credits

Cover: © World Picture News
ABC News/AP/Wide World Photos, 15
AFP/Getty Images, 31
AP/Wide World Photos, 16, 18, 19, 20, 23, 24, 59, 73
Christopher Furlong/Getty Images, 61
Daniel Deme/EPA/Landov, 36
© Darren Staples/CORBIS, 58
Getty Images, 30, 39, 42, 43, 46, 48, 54, 63
Herwig Vergult/EPA/Landov, 74
Ian Hodgson/Reuters/Landov, 55
Mario Tama/Getty Images, 26
Maury Aaseng, 10, 17, 44, 64
Nigel Hine/WENN/Landov, 9
Odd Andersen/Getty Images, 53
Peter Macdiarmid/Getty Images, 33, 51
Philippe Huguen/Getty Images, 35
Photoshot/Landov, 70
© Reuters/CORBIS, 47
Reuters/Landov, 25, 67
Reuters/Paul Hackett/Landov, 69
Scott Barbour/Getty Images, 13
© Sion Touhig/CORBIS, 41
© Stephen Hird/Reuters/CORBIS, 80
Stephen Pond/EPA/Landov, 77
© Toby Melville/Reuters/CORBIS, 29

About the Author

Gail B. Stewart received her undergraduate degree from Gustavus Adolphus College in St. Peter, Minnesota. She did her graduate work in English, linguistics, and curriculum study at the College of St. Thomas and the University of Minnesota. She taught English and reading for more than ten years.

She has written over ninety books for young people, including a series for Lucent Books called The Other America. She has written many books on historical topics, such as World War I and the Warsaw ghetto.

Stewart and her husband live in Minneapolis with their three sons—Ted, Elliot, and Flynn—two dogs, and a cat. When she is not writing, she enjoys reading, walking, and watching her sons play soccer.